Better Homes and

Baths

YOUR GUIDE TO PLANNING AND REMODELING

Better Homes and Gardens® Books
Des Moines, Iowa

Better Homes and Gardens® Books
An Imprint of Meredith® Books

Baths: Your Guide to Planning and Remodeling
Editor: Benjamin W. Allen
Contributing Writer: Linda Mason Hunter
Associate Art Director: Lynda Haupert
Copy Chief: Angela K. Renkoski
Electronic Production Coordinator: Paula Forest
Editorial Assistant: Susan McBroom
Art Assistant: Jennifer Norris
Production Manager: Douglas Johnston
Prepress Coordinator: Marjorie J. Schenkelberg

Meredith® Books
Editor in Chief: James D. Blume
Managing Editor: Christopher Cavanaugh
Editor, Shelter Books: Denise Caringer
Director, New Product Development: Ray Wolf
Vice President, Retail Marketing: Jamie L. Martin

Better Homes and Gardens® Magazine
Editor in Chief: Jean LemMon
Executive Building Editor: Joan McCloskey

Meredith Publishing Group
President, Publishing Group: Christopher Little
Vice President and Publishing Director: John P. Loughlin

Meredith Corporation
Chairman of the Board and Chief Executive Officer: Jack D. Rehm
President and Chief Operating Officer: William T. Kerr
Chairman of the Executive Committee: E. T. Meredith III

Cover photograph: This bath is shown on pages 26 and 27.
Photographs courtesy of: © Laurie Black: Cover, 26, 27. Beth Singer, Photographer: 19. Linda
Mason Hunter: 62, 65. Photographer Steve Hall for Hedrich Blessing, Ltd.: 86 (bath designed by
John Robert Wiltgen).

National and regional remodeling costs on page 79 excerpted with permission from the October
1995 issue of *Remodeling* magazine, © Hanley-Wood, Inc.

Special thanks to Dale Mulfinger of Mulfinger, Susanka, Mahady & Partners, Inc., of Minneapolis,
Minnesota, for his help on this book and his insight on bath design.

All of us at Better Homes and Gardens® Books are dedicated to providing you with information
and ideas you need to enhance your home. We welcome your comments and suggestions about
this book on baths. Write to us at: Better Homes and Gardens® Books, Do-It-Yourself Editorial
Department, RW-240, 1716 Locust St., Des Moines, IA 50309–3023.

Contents

PHASE 1: EXPLORING OPTIONS

Bathroom Basics   4

Gallery of Great Baths   16

Elements of Good Design   32

PHASE 2: NARROWING OPTIONS

Making a Plan   44

Case Studies   62

Budgeting   74

Surface Materials   82

Fixtures   92

PHASE 3: BUILDING

Getting It Done   102

Index and Metric Equivalents   112

About This Guide

Baths: Your Guide to Planning and Remodeling leads you through the process of planning and designing a bathroom. The order of phases and chapters is based on a typical remodeling project. However, your remodeling may vary from this order or you may need to go back and forth through the book as you modify your plans.

Phase 1: Exploring Options provides you with inspirational ideas and general information.

Phase 2: Narrowing Options gives specific information about plans for remodeling, budgeting, and materials and fixtures.

Phase 3: Building tells you what you need to know when you're dealing with contractors.

Bathroom Basics

Before you begin remodeling, determine your needs and educate yourself about your options.

A bathroom at its most basic consists of an enclosed space and some plumbing fixtures. Sounds simple, right? And yet, bathrooms can be among the most complex and challenging parts of a house to design and remodel. Yesterday's gloomy water closets have evolved into today's appealing cleansing and relaxation rooms. Recent trends include sunnier spaces; whirlpool tubs; luxurious showers; two sinks; barrier-free design; improved lighting; more storage for bath accessories and supplies; and even twin bathrooms in master suites.

The best new and remodeled bathrooms reflect the way people live today. Life has speeded up considerably in recent decades, and family members are now under more pressure than ever to get up and out of the house quickly. Smart bathroom design can smooth your way by making efficient use of every available square foot while adding visual interest and beauty.

Renovating or adding a bathroom is one of the best home improvement investments you can make. The main benefit is the added enjoyment and pride of ownership you'll feel while you continue living in your house. You'll also realize benefits if you should decide to sell. An adequate number of eye-catching, fully functioning bathrooms is one of the first things people look for when shopping for a house. Upgrading an old bath or adding a new one may be just what you need to ensure a quick sale. The dollars you spend on a bathroom facelift, expansion, or addition almost certainly will increase the value of your real estate investment.

The key to a successful remodeling is planning. That's what this book is about. It offers you a systematic approach to the phases of bathroom design, materials selection, and construction. Follow the steps in this book, and you can make your dream bath a reality.

➤ *Early remodeling decisions can help get the look you want—such as choosing to keep the wainscoting and pine flooring, then using new wainscoting for the tub surround for a rustic setting.*

Assess Your Wants and Needs

Before rushing into drawing your floor plans and choosing the fixtures, step back and determine exactly what you want and need in a new bathroom. You probably have general ideas about this already, but the more thorough and specific you can be from the outset, the more satisfying the final results will be.

Start by taking detailed stock of your present bathroom situation. Consider everything from surface materials to more fundamental issues, such as layout and location. Perhaps new flooring, wall coverings, countertops, cabinetry, or fixtures would do the trick. Or maybe you'll need to rearrange the layout of an existing bathroom, add onto it, or create an entirely new one. See page 10 for the levels of remodeling you can choose from.

Sometimes a bathroom doesn't work well because it has too much space. This happens most often in houses that were built before the advent of indoor plumbing. When the outdoor privy came indoors, it often was placed in a bedroom or some other space that lacked the right proportions or scale to function as an efficient bathroom. These old-fashioned bathrooms may contain all the essentials yet look and feel awkward in actual use, so they offer many opportunities for improvement.

Wants and needs must always be balanced against the budgetary bottom line. We'll deal with budget matters again later in this chapter (see page 14) and more fully in Phase 2: Budgeting (starting on page 74). For now, just remember not to let your planning decisions get out of touch with financial realities. If you're updating a bath in order to make the house more marketable, don't overdo it. You could lose money by overimproving (spending more than you can realistically hope to recover on resale) or by installing unconventional products or materials. If, on the other hand, you plan to live in your present house for the next 10 years, indulge yourself a little. Remember the trade-off strategy: By choosing, say, stock ceramic tile from a retail outlet as opposed to specialty tile, you'll save money and retain a high resale value. Simple choices can

save money you can apply toward a feature you really want, such as a nice whirlpool tub, a marble vanity top, or deluxe shower hardware.

The following list of questions will help you analyze what you need in a new or renovated bathroom. Understand that these questions are only a beginning—a springboard to get you started in evaluating your particular situation.

Take Stock of Your Existing Bathroom

- Can two people comfortably and conveniently use the bathroom at the same time?
- Do you use the tub for relaxing soaks?
- Is the bathroom just for kids? Do they like using it? Why or why not? Is it child-safe?
- If this is the main family bathroom or a children's bath, is it close to the bedrooms?
- Does the bathroom relate to adjacent rooms the way you would like it to?
- Are there frequent traffic jams in or near the bathroom?
- Is there a door that swings into the traffic path?
- Is the room primarily a shower/bath/toilet area, or is it also a place to shave or apply makeup?
- Are you forever bumping your elbow on a side wall when you brush your teeth?
- Is the toilet visible through an open door?
- Are there enough electrical outlets near the sink and mirror (are they ground-fault circuit interrupter, or GFCI, outlets)?
- Are there places for a towel and a bathrobe close to the shower and/or tub?
- Are there allotted spaces for such items as a laundry hamper, a bathroom scale, towels, bathrobes, and a toilet brush and plunger?
- Is there ample, convenient storage?
- Is the sink of adequate size? Or, would two sinks be better?
- Are the lighting and ventilation adequate?
- Is there a grab bar next to the shower or tub?
- Is there enough counter space?
- Is the bathtub or shower big enough?
- Are there signs of water damage anywhere?

Bath Sizes

Once you've decided what part of the house the bathroom will serve best and who will be using it, the next basic question is, "What type of bathroom am I planning?" To find your answer, inventory the shortcomings of your current bathroom. Keep a running list of your general wants and needs in mind as you start to get more specific about your remodeling plan and what size bathroom you want to create.

Don't rush the process. According to many design experts, you should spend as much time planning and designing your new bathroom as it takes for the construction phase of your project. Take the time to visit real-estate open houses and design shows to gather design ideas, and check out plumbing supply firms for product ideas.

Following are the three basic bath options, along with size requirements for each.

Half Bath

A sink and toilet constitute a half bath, also known as a powder room. Typically, half baths are located on a home's main level, close to the main living areas. They're intended primarily for visitors' use and to provide backup for the main bath. Common dimensions for half baths are 4×5 feet or 3×7 feet. In a pinch, they can be as small as 3×6 or 4½×4½ feet and still work effectively.

Powder rooms are often the most overlooked part of the house. It's tempting to ignore a room that's not used often, but think of your guests and the impressions they'll take away from their visit. Because they are generally small, powder rooms offer an opportunity for fun, offbeat, or lavish decorating. Powder rooms also can pack a lot of convenience in a small space. Adding one can increase your home's value—both as an enjoyable place for your family and as a real estate asset.

Three-Quarter Bath

Equipped with a shower stall instead of a tub, a three-quarter bath can be squeezed into a space that measures 6×6 feet.

If your family prefers showering to bathing, a three-quarter bath could solve your morning traffic jams. Other good uses for this kind of bath include a guest bath, a bathroom for older children, and a backup to the main family bath.

Full Bath

Typically located close to bedrooms, a full bathroom consists of a sink, toilet, and tub. In place of a tub, a full bath may contain a separate tub and shower or a combination of the two. The minimum room size needed to accommodate this full range of fixtures is 5×7 feet. Many different floor plans are possible, though it all depends on your particular wants, needs, and budget.

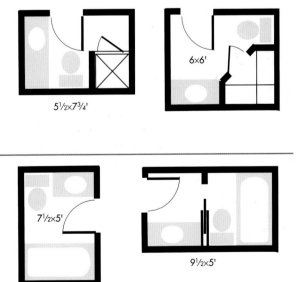

Remodeling Trends

Create a Children's Bath

Children have their own wants and needs that can be met by a bathroom designed especially for them. One possibility is to modify a drab family bath into a colorful, kid-friendly oasis where everything from brushing teeth to scrubbing behind the ears is suffused with fun. Individual sinks, such as those shown, *left*, and dressing areas for each child will help morning and evening routines go more smoothly. Waterproof, easy-to-clean surfaces are naturals here. Safety is another important consideration. Faucets that prevent scalding, appropriately placed grab bars, and slip-resistant surfaces can help prevent accidents.

◄ *Simple accent colors on such places as the walls, cabinet knobs, and accessories can be changed easily when children grow and tastes change.*

Create a Compartmented Bath

In any bathroom that's typically used by more than one person at a time, a few strategically placed walls can make one bathroom function as smoothly as two.

By dividing the room into sections or compartments, two people can use the space at the same time with greater efficiency and an enhanced sense of privacy. The bathroom shown at *left* divides the vanity area, for example, from the tub and encloses the toilet in its own nook. This strategy is especially useful when you want a bathroom that will function better but expanding or creating two separate bathrooms is out of the question.

◄ *Compartmented baths are functional but potentially dark. Here, glass block not only links the two areas but allows in daylight, too. At night, individual ceiling lights for each compartment take over. You also can visually expand a narrow compartment by adding wall-to-wall shelves, as was done here above the toilet.*

▲ *Corner space often can be used more efficiently by angling some of the fixtures. This shower and vanity incorporate angles that allow longer sight lines, giving the bath a more expansive look.*

Create a Master Bath

Not long ago, master bathrooms were considered a luxury. Today, however, master baths are thought of as necessities as retreats from the outside world and amenity-filled places to rejuvenate both body and spirit.

Well-appointed master bathrooms often contain separate areas for bathing, showering, basic grooming, and applying makeup. Sometimes they also incorporate areas for dressing, lounging, and exercise. The most luxurious master baths are divided (or compartmented) into zones variously consisting of a large shower, a whirlpool tub, two sinks, and plenty of storage space. Another zone contains the toilet, which is isolated for privacy. Elegant surfaces made of marble, granite, or a solid-surface material frequently grace master baths. Architectural focal points—perhaps a greenhouse bump-out surrounding the soaking tub or a cathedral ceiling with a skylight—engage the eye.

Another trend in luxury bathrooms is toward the bathroom spa. A spa typically includes a sauna, steam bath, hot tub, and even some exercise equipment. It's best to locate a spa with convenience and privacy in mind. An ideal area is adjacent to the master bedroom/bath.

Levels of Remodeling

Once you've decided what kind of bathroom you want, it's time to plot your strategy for getting it. Can it be done with a simple facelift, will it require adding onto your house, or does it fall somewhere in between? The following five basic remodeling categories are arranged from the least costly to the most.

Facelift

If an existing bathroom works well but needs an infusion of style, it may need only a facelift. This involves re-covering, refinishing, or replacing any or all of the existing wall, floor, ceiling, and countertop surfaces. It also can include replacing the plumbing fixtures and/or adding new lighting, a heat lamp, and an exhaust fan. With the right combination of well-chosen materials, you can make a dramatic change for relatively little money and labor.

Minimal Remodeling

With a few changes to your existing bathroom layout, you can make a small bathroom function and feel like a larger one. A bath as small as 5×8 feet, for example, can be divided into sections by adding a wall, and perhaps a pocket door, to separate the tub (or tub and toilet) from the lavatory. Create a sense of expanded space by adding a large mirror or two, installing recessed or strip lighting fixtures, or raising or vaulting the ceiling. When decorating, keep the colors light and the patterns simple.

Expansion

If space is tight, consider expanding the bathroom into space borrowed from adjoining areas. You may be able to incorporate all or part of a closet, hallway, or bedroom to gain the bathroom space you need. A few extra square feet can make a world of difference.

Finding Space

This option involves carving out space from your home's existing floor plan for a new bathroom. To find the space, look first to rooms that already have plumbing—the kitchen or laundry room, for example. In multistory homes, look to second floor areas above an existing bathroom, kitchen, or laundry room. Often, little nooks can be expanded or hidden spaces opened up as shown in the floor plans, *below*. Make use of space beneath a staircase, for example, or under the eaves in the attic, *opposite*.

Building an Addition

If expanding your current bath or finding space for another one within your home just won't work, you may need to add onto your house. Often a simple extension under a roof overhang can yield enough space for a full bath. Or, adding a 3-foot bump-out may create all the space you need. If you're remodeling on a second or third story, think about making attic space usable by building a dormer. Extra bathrooms and powder rooms can be fitted into surprisingly small spaces and can add considerable value to your house.

Small Baths That Work Big

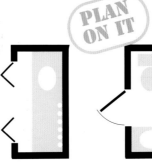

▲ *A makeup center can be installed in an existing closet.*

▲ *This half bath fits under a stairway or in a coat closet.*

▲ *This 4×7-foot closet space still has room for a shower.*

▲ *A half bath in an attic can be a convenient solution if you need to add a bath, because you often can locate it directly above existing plumbing, making tapping into the supply and drain lines an easy matter.*

Plumbing Basics

The whole idea when adding or moving bathroom fixtures is to take maximum advantage of your present plumbing. Replacing old fixtures with new ones in the same location is fairly simple. Installing new plumbing runs (called roughing-in) to place fixtures in new locations requires skill and planning. It also may require a plumbing license, so check with your local building department before doing such work. In any case, when planning to add bathroom fixtures, place them as close as possible to existing plumbing to keep new runs short. If you don't, costs can skyrocket.

Residential plumbing systems are easy to understand. In general, a home plumbing system consists of two networks of pipes. One is the supply system—the pipes that carry water into the house and distribute it to all your plumbing fixtures. The other plumbing network is the drain, waste, and vent (DWV) system, which carries drain water, waste, and harmful gases out of the house. A complete diagram of typical supply and DWV systems is shown *opposite*.

Supply

In the supply system, an underground line from a water source connects to a meter that measures the amount of water entering the house. Next to the meter is a shutoff valve that, when closed, stops water from flowing into the house. The main supply line branches into two lines—one for cold water and one for hot. The cold-water supply line feeds the network of supply pipes throughout the house. The hot-water supply line goes to your water heater. From there, the hot-water pipes run parallel with the cold-water pipes to serve various fixtures and faucets.

Your home's water-supply system is pressurized, but the drain-waste system depends on gravity. These pipes also are connected to vents, which allow sewer gases to escape harmlessly up a chimneylike vent stack. Plumbing vents also allow the entire DWV system to maintain atmospheric pressure so the flow of waste water is not affected by vacuums, back-pressure, or siphoning.

Drains and Vents

Because each new or moved bathroom fixture must connect with a main soil stack, you must know the locations of your main vents, then determine a route for attaching new vent lines to them. You may live in an area where building codes specify the size and general conformation of drainage, waste, and vent lines. So, once again, consult local codes and hire a licensed professional plumber, if necessary. Unless you're an accomplished do-it-yourselfer, it's best to leave major plumbing jobs to a professional.

Rerouting plumbing is much easier if the house has a basement or crawlspace. If the house is built on a concrete slab, adding new baths or fixtures may require demolishing part of the slab to gain access to main plumbing lines. Also check to see if your water heater has enough capacity to meet the added hot-water demand. You may want to add another water heater.

Plumbing Design

When planning a bathroom, keep these basic rules and principles of plumbing in mind:

■ Each bathroom fixture must have a drain with a trap—a curved pipe that always retains a little water in it as a seal to prevent sewage gases from coming through the drain pipe and escaping into the house.

■ Beyond the trap, each drain must be connected to a vent pipe that either goes directly up through the roof or connects to another vent stack. Plumbing vents (also called soil stacks) run from the lowest part of the system clear up to the roof. For cosmetic reasons, it's best to run vent stacks up through the back side of the roof, not the front.

■ The drain-waste lines run to the lower parts of the house then exit to a city sewer system or a septic tank.

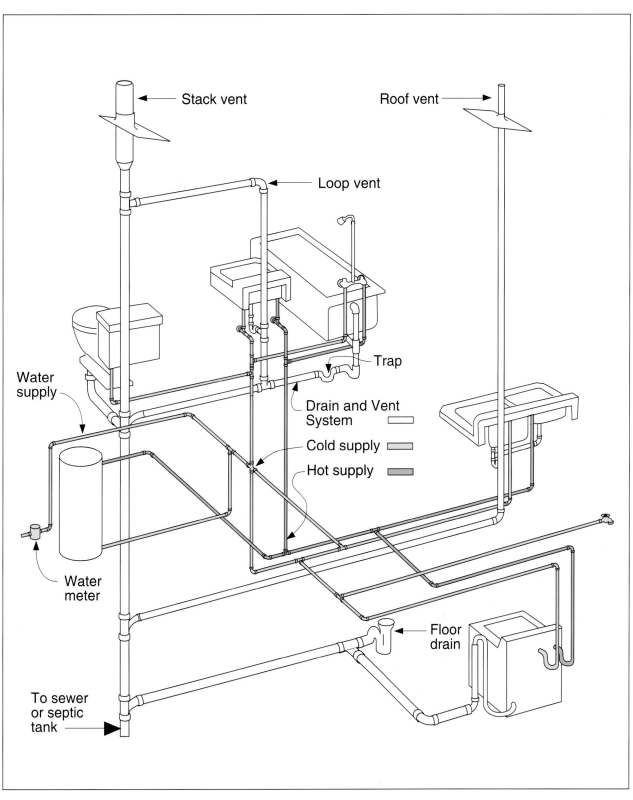

Stack vent

Roof vent

Loop vent

Trap

Water
supply

Drain and Vent
System

Cold supply

Hot supply

Water
meter

Floor
drain

To sewer
or septic
tank

Typical plumbing system

Design Trends

When designing a new bathroom, think function, comfort, and luxury. The following tips will help you create a bathroom that will serve you well for the next 10 years.

Storage. Reduce clutter by storing as many bathroom and grooming supplies as possible. Use cabinetry, vanities, and shelves that provide maximum storage in a minimum of space. Wire storage systems can do wonders for organizing cabinets. If you can, incorporate a closet or large cabinet just for towels and other bulky items. If you follow the trend toward having two sinks in a full bath, then you'll probably want two medicine cabinets. Or, you may want to place an expanse of fixed mirror above both sinks and store items below in the vanity. Also consider buying or building a storage unit that makes use of space above the toilet.

Materials. Materials that require frequent maintenance are out of fashion. Look for floor, cabinet, countertop, and wall surfaces that resist stains and clean up in a snap. Natural materials such as polished marble and granite and solid-surface materials such as Corian cost more, but pay you back with stain resistance and durability.

Shrinking the bath. Don't think that the only way to improve a bath is to make it larger; instead, go for cozy, but don't forgo the luxuries. Most people find they don't have time to fill a whirlpool tub very often. Even so, you may want one in your remodeling plan because of the sizzle it can add at resale time. Avoid the morning rush-hour crunch by including dual sinks and a shower that is separate from the tub.

Light. Bring in all the natural light you can with skylights, glass doors, wall cutouts, glass block, and windows. Fill in the shadows with built-in lighting fixtures.

Openness. Mirrors, glass block, large windows, skylights, and open or glass-enclosed showers will create a sense of openness, making any space appear larger than its actual dimensions.

Budget Matters

Until you have planned your bathroom down to the last detail, you won't be able to pin down costs. "Budgeting," pages 74 to 81, will guide you through this process. In the meantime, keep budgetary realities firmly in mind throughout your planning. It's important right from the beginning to establish a ballpark dollar figure that you're willing to spend on remodeling. By setting a firm budgetary goal, then doing your best at every stage to stick to it, you'll probably end up with a more value-packed bathroom.

To help you begin, there are a few general numbers to serve as guides. If you select medium-cost fixtures (for example, a $300 toilet, a $300 sink, and a $650 porcelain-on-steel bathtub) and use a moderately priced ceramic tile on the floor, you can refurbish an existing small bathroom for $3,500 to $5,000. Expect a nicely remodeled, well-appointed powder room to cost between $4,000 and $5,000. If you plan a complete overhaul of a full bath, count on spending at least $5,000. Of course you can realize considerable savings if you do much of the work yourself.

Special materials and items that require skilled labor will run the price up. If your budget is limited, stay away from colored fixtures. They cost 20 to 30 percent more than white fixtures and may look dated in a few years. White fixtures are easier to match when decorating, too.

In general, you'll get the best return on your home improvement investment by:
- hiring a professional designer
- making the space light and bright
- using high-quality materials
- decorating with classic colors
- installing white fixtures
- wisely incorporating the recent trends in bathroom design.

▲ *Think light and bright. Bright lights, neutral colors, a see-through shower door, and a large mirror give this bathroom a feeling of expansiveness even though it's only 5 feet square.*

Gallery of Great Baths

Use the following baths for ideas to create your dream bath.

Close your eyes and imagine your new bathroom. What overall impression does it convey? Is it basic and functional? Dramatic? Traditional? Is it flashy or restrained, sophisticated or rustic? If your new bathroom were a person whom you'd just met, what words would you use to describe it?

The "personality" you're imagining is the sum of many details—fixtures, lighting, cabinets, flooring, paint, accessories, and so on. The essence of a great bathroom resides in these details. Before you can fill them in, however, you need to have a vision of the whole.

This chapter contains a collection of photos designed to help you develop your bathroom's personality. Look at the pictures without comparing them to your style. Just look to get ideas. Use these images to supplement (or to begin) the design notebook suggested on page 43.

Then look again, more critically this time. Ask yourself what elements give each bathroom its distinct personality. Let the design ideas in our photo gallery help you imagine your own dream bath in increasingly vivid detail.

➤ *Gleaming white fixtures stand like sculpture against a neutral palette in this tranquil master bathroom. The pedestal sink is an antique, the claw-foot tub a reproduction. For a twist, these ceramic tiles are laid on the diagonal.*

◀ *A subtle wall treatment of cream-colored diamonds painted on an off-white background gives this room its soft glow.*

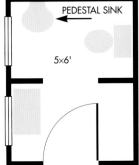

◄ *Located near this home's front entry, this compact powder room provides space for a pedestal sink, toilet, and a sitting area—a welcoming little retreat for guests.*

PEDESTAL SINK

5×6'

Powder Rooms:
Small but Sumptuous

A black pedestal sink inspired the design for this 5×6-foot powder room. The sitting area is decorated in warm green tones, with woodland-scene wallpaper and a painted faux-marble woodwork treatment. The marbled effect continues on the washroom woodwork, but the wall covering changes to a bold stripe. The pedestal sink, silk

drapery, and fancy faucet were close-out bargains.

Before it was remodeled, this bath contained a dated blue sink and toilet; the floor was covered with a drab carpet glued over blue tile. The only structural changes made during the remodeling were the windows: Two new casement units replaced a drafty pair of double-hung windows.

Narrow Your Choices

◄ *A few traditional accessories—such as the heirloom silver bowl and beveled mirror with its antique frame—warm up and soften the contemporary style of this small powder room.*

Just off a dining room hallway, this powder room offered a daunting decorating challenge because it was so long and narrow. The homeowners (who are interior designers) hung art in the 5×10-foot room, creating points of interest that break up the boxcar effect. A curvy onyx countertop, round silver nickel sink, conical light fixtures, and angled walls all blend to make a virtue of the room's size and shape.

Two of the bathroom walls are painted a deep greenish gray to set off paintings and photographs. The remaining walls and ceiling are painted white so the space doesn't give the feeling of being closed in.

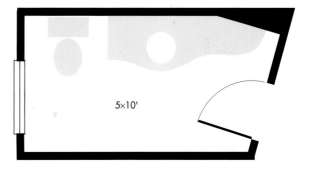

5×10'

Sense Appeal

◄ The custom-made blond mirror frame and the wall sconce add to the Craftsman-type theme echoed in the copper towel bar for an overall sunny, sensuous Arts and Crafts look.

5×8'

A refreshing mix of colors, materials, and texture turned this ordinary 5×8-foot half bath into something special. To make the textured walls, the homeowners mixed hues of yellow and pink into joint compound, then troweled it on thickly. After the compound had partially hardened, they knocked off the peaks with a drywall knife. Then they applied a protective coat of acrylic semigloss glaze. To enrich the tactile theme in the bath, they surfaced the countertop and backsplash with rough granite.

Industrial-grade copper pipe nearly encircles the room at countertop level, ensuring that a towel is always within reach. The surface behind the bar is painted with a verdigris finish, mimicking aged copper.

Kids' Baths: Sibling Harmony

▲ *Reusing the original bathroom's vintage pedestal sinks, medicine cabinets, and tub helped keep costs down.*

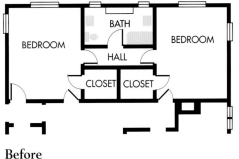

Before

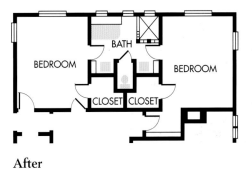

After

When updating a cramped, dated bathroom situated between their two sons' bedrooms, the homeowners of this bath requested separate but equal facilities. To enlarge the existing bath to a 12×10-foot room, they incorporated a hallway previously connecting the two bedrooms and bumped a new toilet compartment into space stolen from closets.

Rearranging the fixtures so the sinks are on either side of the toilet compartment and the bath occupies a corner and adding a shower made the most of the space. New doors close off the bath from each of the bedrooms.

Black and white ceramic tile on the floor and walls provides a lively background that will remain classic even as the boys' tastes change.

As They Grow

◄ Well-suited to the bathing needs of a child, this tub alcove includes a showerhead that, when teamed with a shower curtain on a tension rod, will come in handy as the child gets older. Equally accommodating is the simple tile, which can adapt to new schemes as tastes change.

The key qualities of a successful children's bath are safety and durability.

Safety begins with materials selection. Experts recommend against slippery, high-gloss flooring finishes. Instead, choose a nonslip floor surface such as ceramic tile with a matte finish. Smaller tiles, when installed, have more grout lines per square foot. Grout is not slippery, so smaller tiles can enhance bathroom safety.

A durable children's bathroom not only holds up under daily use for years, but it also should work well through all the stages of childhood. Scale the bath to fit the needs of adults, but at the same time, make it feel comfortable and appealing to children.

Pick standard-height counters, for example, while including a built-in stepping stool so children can easily wash their hands and brush their teeth. Similarly, a second, lower set of towel bars can help children pick up after themselves without compromising grown-up requirements. In the tub, install a standard-height showerhead, but include a hand-held sprayer, attached at spout level, for easy rinsing and cleanup.

The decorative elements of a kids' bath should be equally adaptable. Keep the background simple; select an easy-care, glossy paint or a scrubbable, strippable wallpaper. This will make for easier cleanups now and quick cosmetic changes later.

Consider matching a timeless wallpaper—a simple striped pattern, for example—with a whimsical border that's appropriate for your child's age. When the time comes, you easily can replace the border with a more refined pattern. Bathroom accessories, from towels to toothbrush holders, constitute another group of easy-to-change, inexpensive options.

➤ *Easily removed wallpaper and whimsical accessories create a fun, oceanlike room for a preschooler. The mirror tiles bordering the window make the room seem larger than it is.*

Make Your Bath Kid-Friendly

Protect your child against potential dangers in the bathroom by heeding the safety precautions on page 42 and taking these extra steps:

■ Keep washcloths and toys at tubside so you won't be tempted to leave your child unattended in the bath.

■ A cushion around the tub spout, as well as edge and corner cushions on cabinets, can help prevent cuts and bruises.

■ Install childproof locks on all cabinets. Even the toilet lid should have a latch.

■ Use only nonbreakable drinking tumblers in a bathroom. Store them where kids can reach them without making a precarious climb.

■ Add slip-resistant strips in front of the sink and tub. Anchor area rugs with nonslip pads or double-faced carpet tape.

■ Block all electrical outlets with safety covers or plugs. The outlets, as in all baths, should be GFCI outlets.

■ Make sure grab bars inside the bathtub and shower stall are low enough for children to use.

■ Choose faucets and handles that are easy to use and have rounded edges. Also, cover the tap with an inflated plastic or sponge case.

■ Locate towel bars or rings 6 inches or less from entrances to a tub or shower so children don't have to reach too far for them.

Full Baths:
Magnificent Makeover

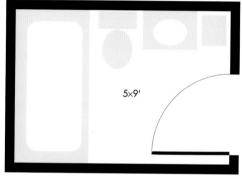

5×9'

▲ A finishing touch to remodeling this bath was to replace a stingy oval mirror with a large framed one to create a room-expanding effect.

This modest-size (5×9-foot) full bath is visible from the front door of a small home. Formerly drab and outdated, a few bold strokes transformed it into a beautiful retreat. Contrary to some friends' advice, the owner repainted the walls, ceiling, and vanity a dark burgundy. Instead of making it feel closed in and tiny, the deep hue seems to blur the bath's boundaries.

Draping the shower/tub in rich folds is a muslin curtain—a simple, sophisticated, low-cost idea. Carved wooden shelves, traditional framed prints, ginger jars, and other pieces of blue and white china add an elegantly furnished look.

To make a similar shower curtain, purchase good cotton muslin with a permanent-press finish (costs about $4 per yard depending on the fabric's width). Double the tub's width to create a generously draped effect, and add to the length to make the fabric puddle on the floor. To finish the job and keep water in its place, pair your curtain with a vinyl shower-curtain liner.

Turn-of-the-Century Charm

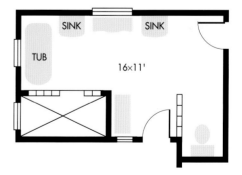

▲ *A judicious use of glass block, together with the arrangement of windows, mirrors, and light fixtures, lightens the traditional elements with a touch of modern style.*

The trick in bringing a traditional look into this bath was to pick the right elements but not go overboard. The homeowners planned their bath around two favorite antique furniture pieces—an armoire and a dresser. The contractor tracked down a reconditioned claw-foot tub. The two pedestal sinks appear to be of the same vintage as the tub, though they are actually reproductions.

Towels air out on an antique quilt rack. The perfect wrapping for this period package is the beaded wainscoting, painted a creamy white.

▲ *Overscaled elements such as the limestone tiles, large casement windows, pedestal sink, and beveled medicine cabinet add a sophisticated, contemporary tone.*

Earthy Delights

Simple, natural materials give this master bath a fresh, earthy elegance. The walls are tinted plaster, the floor is covered with limestone squares, and the sconces are carved from alabaster. Simple wood trim, painted white, adorns the windows; white ceramic tile with sand-colored grout encases the shower.

The resulting bath has an honest, forthright farmhouse feel, yet it's far from naive. The sink and toilet have sculptural, lyrical lines, making them design elements in the otherwise sparsely furnished bath.

Large windows offer a tranquil mountain view from each of the functional elements (sink, tub, and toilet). The whirlpool tub, set in a limestone-tiled platform, also benefits from unobstructed outdoor views in two directions.

➤ *The slim baseboard heating unit, which supplies hot-water radiant heat, adds to the room's personality, as does the warming rack for towels above the tub.*

➤ *Occupying a private nook, the low-consumption, low-profile toilet is shielded by the shower. In the 3×3-foot shower stall, a handheld showerhead adjusts to the user's needs.*

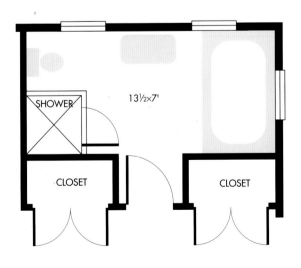

SHOWER

13½×7'

CLOSET

CLOSET

A Bath Built for Two

Master baths are, almost by definition, supposed to accommodate two users at once. Efficiency, for those busy mornings when minutes count, is just as important as a sense of pampered luxury. Actual space requirements will vary according to what features you choose. Some of today's most popular amenities in master baths include:

■ two vanities, each with its own sink and mirror, or one long vanity that is equipped with two sinks

■ a toilet that occupies its own enclosed or semienclosed space for added privacy

■ dual showerheads, one fitted at each end of a double shower, or both a shower and a tub so two people can bathe at once

■ customized fixtures to fit both users; for example, dual showerheads can be installed at different levels, and vanity heights can vary up or down from the standard 32 inches

■ personalized built-in storage for each user

■ easy access to the dressing area and separate walk-in closets.

▲ *Two sinks allow simultaneous access for grooming. For users of different heights, the shower has two showerheads mounted at different levels.*

Pros and Cons of Two-Person Whirlpool Tubs

Soothing sore muscles or frazzled nerves in a bubbling tub made for two is definitely appealing. But will you use it? Some couples have discovered they rarely take the time to soak together. Others conclude that soaking solo is actually more relaxing, so the extra water and room required for a double-size tub often are wasted. Keep in mind that large whirlpools take a long time to fill and may require added structural support below because they are enormously heavy when full. Also, a big tub is proportionately more difficult and time-consuming to clean.

▲ *A grab bar next to the toilet and a cantilevered sink help wheelchair users maneuver.*

▲ *To accommodate wheelchairs, this bathroom has been outfitted with an oversize, doorless shower stall.*

Bathrooms for the Disabled

Bathrooms for people with particular needs require knowledgeable planning. When implementing your plan, remember that such bathrooms need not look institutional. Begin the planning process with an inventory of the intended user's skills, focusing not on disabilities, but capabilities, likes, and tastes. What can the person do? What does he or she like to do?

The first priority in bathrooms intended for people who use wheelchairs is plenty of room for access and maneuvering. Barrier-free bathrooms are usually larger than average. Provide for an open area within the bathroom that's at least 5 feet in diameter to allow for easy turning. Also provide 4 feet of clear space in front of each fixture, as well as between the sink and the toilet, if both fixtures share the same wall. These spaces also will allow room for a caregiver, if needed.

Make doorways 3 feet wide so a wheelchair can pass through. The bathroom door must swing outward rather than inward and should be fitted with a lever-type handle, not a knob.

Specify a vanity designed for use from a wheelchair. Plan for a sit-down dressing table with a 31-inch-high countertop and at least 30 inches of clear knee space underneath so a chair can pull in close.

The shower stall should have no threshold that would impede the entrance and exit of a wheelchair. The stall should measure at least 4 feet square, and its opening should be at least 36 inches wide. Install the control valves and showerheads at two different heights, or include a hand-held nozzle that can be used from a seated position. A built-in seat in the shower, along with a sturdy grab bar, can provide extra comfort and utility.

Other features of an accessible bath include grab rails mounted on reinforced walls beside the tub and toilet (and bidet, if there is one), faucets designed to reduce the risk of scalding, a telephone, and lower light switches (48 inches off the ground puts them within reach of wheelchair users and kids).

Vanities: Room to Groom

A plain oak vanity cabinet with an integral sink and countertop may be the most common component in remodeled bathrooms today, but it's not your only option. Less conventional alternatives solve space and design challenges while offering a distinctive look.

▲ *If you have plenty of storage space, consider leaving out one set of cabinets to form a cozy spot to sit and groom in front of the mirror.*

▲ *Pedestal sinks take up little floor space so they can be placed in unusual spots. This antique shelf stand with brass sink found its niche in an attic dormer.*

◀ *Nicely nostalgic, this vanity is modeled after the shape of old pedestal sinks and made to look like furniture. Ribbed glass covers energy-efficient fluorescent lighting around the mirror.*

Decorating Ideas

Pairing light and dark colors tends to make a room appear smaller and more closed in. To help a small room look as large as possible, choose colors that are similar in value—that is, all light or all dark colors.

Develop a Color Scheme

Creating a good color palette for your bathroom can be a challenge, but there's nothing forbidding or mysterious about it. The following general guidelines will help.

▉ For the sake of continuity, carry your home's overall personality into the bath.

▉ Link the bath with adjoining rooms by matching color values (that is, the colors' darkness or lightness) as well as actual hues. For example, if the trim in the hall outside the bath is painted a high-gloss creamy white, consider using that color somewhere in the bath.

▉ Most successful color schemes use a minimum of three and a maximum of six colors. Three-color schemes consist of a main color (the prevalent color used on most surfaces), a secondary color (often used on cabinets, trim, and/or some wall or ceiling surfaces), and an accent color (the least-used color to provide interest, variety, and balance). The accent is often the brightest or darkest color in a scheme; use it in at least three places (or on one major design element) to establish a definite presence.

▉ Give thought to the color of every component: walls, ceiling, window and door trim, wainscoting or chair rail (if any), floor, furniture, counters, fixtures, curtains, accessories.

▉ When determining your color placement, decide what you want the main focus of the room to be. Consider that the eye is attracted first to the lightest color. If the walls aren't the main focus, they should not be painted the lightest color.

▉ White (including ivory and cream) fixtures are not only less expensive, but they also are easier to clean than dark fixtures.

▉ White comes in many tones, and choosing from among them can be tough. Decide if you want a cool white or a warm white, then choose one specific hue. Match all the white or off-white elements so various tones won't be competing with each other.

▉ If you use the bathroom for applying makeup, choose lighter versions of the colors of the clothes that look good on you. The lighter colors reflect flattering light, allowing you to get your makeup colors correct.

▉ Countertop colors that keep their good looks are lighter midtones, grays, and beiges. Dark colors have poor reflective qualities, solids tend to show marks, and white shows stains.

▉ White cabinets can make a small bath seem larger. Dark cabinets have the opposite effect. Use dark cabinets only in a well-lit room.

Planning a Cosmetic Center

▉ Plan for enough plug-ins. If you have two curling irons and a hair dryer, you'll need more than one outlet.

▉ Put everything in its place. Purchase drawer organizers for cosmetics and hooks for hanging your hair dryer and curling iron.

▉ Light it right. If possible, light the cosmetic center to duplicate the lighting in the place where you're preparing to spend the most time.

That is, if you work in a setting with fluorescent lighting, your makeup center should have fluorescent lighting. The best makeup centers allow users to switch from one type of light to another but these can be expensive.

▉ Plan the proper distance between the mirror and you. When applying eye makeup or lipstick, it's hard to get close enough to the vanity mirror, so supplement it with a hand mirror.

▉ Place the center out of high-traffic areas so you're not jostled as you apply your makeup.

Elements of Good Design

Let form follow function as you choose the design of your new bath.

Armed with answers to the big, basic questions, you're ready to start modifying your project with the realities of bath design. By applying the fundamentals of good design, you avoid creating a bath with a new set of problems you hadn't expected.

Take some time to work through some of the physical constraints fixtures place on design and how concerns of privacy, ventilation, water usage, lighting, storage, and safety can all influence the bath you create.

If you're unsure of your final design, by all means consult with a professional designer (see page 43) so that you're sure your plan is the right one for you. Professional designers often can quickly solve design problems because they may have run into the same problem when designing for someone else's remodeling project.

▲ *Knowing the details of bath design can help you design the perfect bath. Placing lights on either side of the mirror rather than above provides good light for applying cosmetics or shaving.*

➤ *This built-for-two bath was planned down to the last detail. Eye-level storage on both sides of the partition between the vanity sinks provides space for shaving supplies, dryers, and toiletry items. A tiled pedestal between the sinks provides extra space for towels, as does a shelf-lined box built into the wall.*

Plumbing Layout

When placing fixtures in your bathroom layout, think about how they're used and in what order. The sink, for example, should be positioned closest to the door, because it's the last stop in most bathroom routines. Having to squeeze by other fixtures on your way in and out the door can be inconvenient. The toilet, tub, and/or shower can be farther from the door and enclosed in separate compartments for greater privacy, if you wish.

How many "wet walls," or walls that contain plumbing pipes, will there be in your bathroom? The fewer wet walls you have, the less costly your plumbing bill will be. One-wall layouts, with fixtures arranged along a single wall, are the simplest and require the fewest plumbing fittings. Keep in mind, however, that design possibilities are limited with a one-wall layout, and floor space may not be used efficiently.

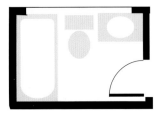

One-Wall Layout
A design with supply and drain pipes located within one wall is more efficient but limits your design possibilities.

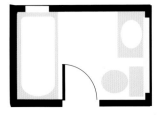

Two-Wall Layout
A design with plumbing in two walls requires more plumbing work but offers more floor area and storage space around the sink.

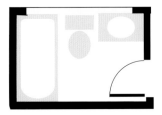

Three-Wall Layout
Three-wall layouts offer the most design flexibility, but they require more space and more complex plumbing systems.

(Bright yellow in the floor diagrams *above* indicates walls with plumbing.)

Minimum Clearances

It's tempting (and often necessary) to squeeze bathrooms into spaces not much larger than a phone booth. What can be forgotten amid all the squeezing and creative layout planning is the human factor—the need, that is, for human elbows, knees, hips, shoulders, and heads to be able to move freely and comfortably within the allotted space.

Based on average human measurements and needs, professional designers have developed recommendations for minimum clearances around doors, fixtures, cabinets, and other common bathroom features. Many of these measurements are recommended by the National Kitchen and Bath Association. The following figures are recommended minimums; allow more space if the fit seems too tight for any of the bathroom's intended users.

■ Doorways should be 32 inches wide, and walkways should be a minimum of 36 inches wide.

■ Plan a minimum of 15 inches from the sink's center to any side wall. To make tasks such as washing hair more comfortable, allow 18 inches on each side.

■ If you install two sinks in the same counter, allow 30 inches, centerline to centerline, between them. Allow at least 8 inches between the edge of a sink and the end of the counter.

■ At least 8 inches should separate the top of the vanity backsplash from the bottom of the medicine cabinet or mirror.

■ Allow at least 16 inches from the center of the toilet to any obstruction, fixture, or equipment on either side. For clearance in front of the toilet, provide an open floor space of 48×48 inches. A good 16 inches of that floor space should extend to each side of the toilet's centerline. Allow at least 1 inch between the back of the water tank and the wall behind it.

■ Position the toilet-paper holder 6 inches beyond the front of the seat with the roller 26 inches above the floor.

■ Minimum interior shower dimensions are 34×34 inches, but most people prefer it roomier.

■ Swinging shower doors must open into the bathroom, away from the shower's interior.

■ Standard height for vanities is 30 to 32 inches. Adjust height upward for tall users. In bathrooms with two vanities, one can be 30 to 34 inches high and the other can be 34 to 42 inches high.

■ Toilets isolated in a separate compartment should occupy a space 36 inches wide by 66 inches deep, with a swing-out or pocket door. Dividing walls are normally about 6 inches thick (including trim at the bottom of both sides), so allow space for them.

Small Space, Big Function

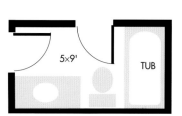

▲ This small half bath could fit in a former closet, mudroom, or laundry area.

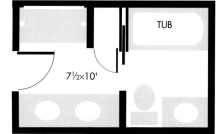

▲ Though it measures only 5×7 feet, this bathroom contains a generous, full-length countertop for grooming and storage.

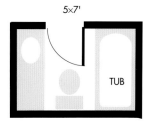

▲ As this floor plan demonstrates, with careful planning, you can fit top-of-the-line fixtures into a modest space.

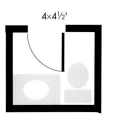

▲ This full bath is accessible from both a bedroom and a hallway.

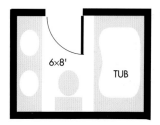

▲ Multifunctional, this compartmented bath meets the needs of an entire family.

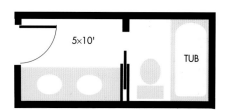

▲ Designed for two people to use simultaneously, this bath has a sliding door to add greater privacy within a limited space.

Privacy

No matter how large or small, the bathroom at its best is a sanctuary of privacy. What feels private to some people may feel uncomfortable to others. Appropriate thresholds of privacy can vary from one type of bathroom to another. A powder room, for example, will have different privacy requirements than a master bath with views of a secluded backyard.

In any case, you'll probably want window coverings for any large expanses of glazing. Avoid heavy fabrics that will soak up moisture. Quick-drying cotton is best, though you may need a liner to avoid transparency. Other options include venetian blinds, miniblinds, and pull-down shades. Don't use wooden blinds or shutters unless your bath has excellent ventilation to get rid of moisture.

Glass block allows in light while obscuring views. It can be used to make internal partition walls (such as shower enclosures) or as a fixed glazing material for window openings. Some kinds of glass block distort views and conserve heat more than others, so choose a pattern that makes you feel comfortable.

Narrow, horizontal windows placed high in the wall offer another possible solution to the light-versus-privacy problem. Remember, just because you can't see out doesn't mean someone else can't see in. A high window in, say, a first-floor bath may be within view of a neighbor's second floor.

In addition to visual privacy, acoustic privacy is a concern in bathrooms. The whir of a ventilating fan can act as welcome white noise, drowning out other sounds. Insulating the bathroom walls also helps. Look in home centers for insulation and wallboard fasteners that are specifically designed to deaden sound.

Ventilation

Bathrooms generate large amounts of humidity. Without a designated means of escape, moisture will build up and penetrate walls, ceilings, floors, and countertops. Mildew thrives, wall coverings curl, paint peels, fixtures rust, and wood (possibly including structural framing) rots.

Because you can't always open a window, your bath should have a ventilating fan that expels moisture, odors, aerosol sprays, and household cleaners. It's important to find a fan that's up to the job.

How Does It Rate?

The Home Ventilating Institute recommends that your exhaust fan be able to expel and replace the entire volume of air in your bathroom eight times per hour. A fan's ability to move air is measured in cubic feet per minute (cfm).

To determine the minimum cfm rating for an exhaust fan, calculate the bathroom's volume in cubic feet (length×width×height), multiply this by 8 (the desired number of air exchanges per hour), and divide the resulting number by 60 (the number of minutes in an hour). Let's say, for example, that your bathroom is 14 feet long, 10 feet wide, and has a 9-foot ceiling. Applying the formula, your calculation would look like this: (14×10×9×8)/60 = 168 cfm). Your building code may specify where the fan must be placed, so check with local authorities before making your final plans.

When shopping for a ventilation fan, also consider how loud it is. Bathroom fans are noise-rated based on units of measurement called sones. The lower the sone rating, the quieter the fan will run.

Optional Features

Beyond their various cfm and sone ratings, bathroom exhaust fans come with combinations of other features. The simplest units have an exhaust fan only. Some of today's more popular models include a built-in light or heater. Top-of-the-line models may come equipped with humidity or motion sensors that turn the fan on and off when humidity reaches a certain level or when someone enters the room. Most bathroom fans have only one speed, although multiple-speed models are available.

Installation

Your exhaust fan should be located close to the shower or bathtub, or high on an exterior wall opposite the bathroom door. Try to keep the ductwork as short and straight as possible. If the exhaust duct will have to twist and turn its way over a long distance, buy a fan with a larger capacity. It's also a good idea to wrap the exhaust duct with some insulation in order to reduce condensation inside it.

The best location for the exhaust fan's outlet is a matter of opinion. Most experts agree that the fan should be vented directly to the outdoors, not into the attic. The best options are to go straight through an exterior wall or straight up through a cap on the roof. Venting the fan to a downward-facing grill in a soffit under the eaves is less than ideal. Some experts say this can cause potentially serious moisture problems.

Water Usage

Within living memory, indoor running water was a luxury. Today, we take it for granted. Yet clean, fresh water is a limited resource, and there are easy ways to avoid wasting it.

Conservation

Toilet flushes account for as much as 40 percent of the typical family's indoor water usage. A family of four can easily flush more than 100 gallons a day down the toilet. To reduce this number to a minimum, all states now require that newly installed toilets be low-flow fixtures. Most current models use around 1.6 gallons per flush (older toilets generally flush about 3.5 gallons with some using up to 5 gallons). With increasing demands on municipal water supplies and the resulting rise in water bills, buying an efficient model pays in the long run.

Showers are another heavy water user. Regulations now restrict newly installed shower-heads to an output of 2.5 gallons of water per minute. That's 30 to 60 percent less than the average shower output before January 1994, when the new law went into effect. The technology of water-saving showerheads has improved to the point where many of today's low-cost models seem just as generous with water as their older, high-consuming counterparts.

Flow-restricting aerators on sink faucets aid conservation still further. Both low-flow shower-heads and faucet aerators are available in hardware stores and home centers.

Hard Water

Water that contains significant amounts of iron, sulfur, manganese, and other mineral impurities commonly is referred to as "hard." Hard water can irritate the skin, causing itching and dryness (especially in the winter). Just as annoying, soap and shampoo refuse to lather, and unsightly deposits form on fixtures.

To test your water for hardness, draw off a pint into a bottle, add 10 drops of dishwashing liquid, cap the bottle, and shake well. If the solution foams readily, your water is relatively soft. If you see a curdlike film instead of foam, consider investing in a water softener. Softer water means you will need less soap for bathing and your plumbing system will work more smoothly because your water heater, pipes, showerheads, and faucets won't collect the corrosive scale that hard water causes.

Lighting

The current trend in lighting is toward larger, sunnier baths, and today's top bathroom designers are placing more emphasis on artificial lighting as well. A single, small lighting fixture protruding from the middle of the ceiling won't do anymore. Alternative sources of general lighting include recessed ceiling fixtures or indirect lighting that bounces off the ceiling or walls. In addition to good general lighting, you'll probably want task lights for all mirrors, separate compartments, the tub, and the shower.

How you choose and arrange these light fixtures depends on the size and layout of your bathroom. It also depends on your color scheme: Bright colors reflect and enhance lighting effects; dark hues absorb and subdue them.

Once you've established a strategy for general illumination, concentrate on task lighting.

Lighting a Mirror

Small or large, a bathroom typically functions as a grooming center. For this reason, you want the area in front of the mirror to be evenly illuminated and free of shadows.

Experts' Insight

When planning a lighting scheme for your bathroom, follow these guidelines to ensure adequate general lighting:

Surface-mounted fixtures: Install bulbs that emit 1 watt of incandescent or ⅓ to ½ watt of fluorescent light per square foot.

Recessed fixtures: Install bulbs that emit 2½ to 4 watts of incandescent light or ½ watt of fluorescent light per square foot.

To do this, place light sources in such a way that light comes at you from above, below, and both sides. This technique, called cross-lighting, effectively eliminates shadows. If you have light coming only from above, it hits your eyebrows, causing shadows beneath your eyes—not an encouraging sight first thing every morning.

Start by installing a fixture that casts light just over the front edge of the sink and countertop. If you choose a light-colored countertop, more light will reflect up onto your face. Then add more lights centered on each side of the mirror.

If you choose to illuminate the mirror with fluorescent fixtures, look for tubes designed for vanity illumination or tubes that produce daylight-spectrum light (the light from standard fluorescent tubes can be cold and harsh—acceptable, perhaps, for office or shop lighting but less than ideal for makeup application). Use one 24-inch, 20-watt tube on each side of the mirror. Above the mirror (or on the ceiling), use two 24-inch, 20-watt tubes or a 32-watt circle light.

If you choose fixtures that require incandescent lightbulbs, one good option is to mount one wall fixture or pendant lamp on each side of the mirror. These side lights each should contain two 60-watt or 75-watt bulbs. If the ceiling fixture is round, it should be at least 12 inches in diameter and contain a bulb or bulbs rated at a total of 100 to 120 watts.

Larger mirrors—including those that are 36 or more inches wide—may demand a different approach. If you follow the guidelines above, you may find that the center of the mirror is a bit dark. To avoid this, use more powerful overhead light fixtures, and make sure they cover the mirror's full width. One effective option is a double row of recessed ceiling fixtures over the vanity.

Small powder rooms typically require one light above the mirror, a fixture on each side of the mirror, and one ceiling light directed toward the front edge of the vanity countertop.

▶ *Incandescent halogen lighting helps turn this previously dull powder room into something out of the ordinary. Smoked-glass inserts frame the mirror for added effect.*

Bath and Shower Lights

In an enclosed shower or tub area, most codes call for enclosed, vapor-proof downlights. Use caution when positioning them, however; you don't want to look right into the light when you're lying in the tub. An infrared heat lamp mounted just outside the tub or shower will help avoid chilly exits. All switches should be located at least 6 feet from the tub and shower.

Stall Lights

In toilet compartments, plan on installing a centered ceiling fixture that uses one 60- to 75-watt incandescent bulb or one 30- to 40-watt fluorescent tube.

The Right Light

Most experts recommend using incandescent bulbs in the bathroom, because the light they produce has natural, complexion-flattering properties. But incandescent bulbs also produce a good deal of heat that's often unwanted. Compact fluorescent fixtures are a good alternative. They demand far less electricity per lumen (a measurement of light intensity), and the tubes render a warm, pleasing spectrum of colors.

Consider using a dimmer switch for your bathroom's overall lighting. (Fluorescents generally don't work with dimmer switches.) This will allow you to adjust the light to suit your needs and moods. Dimmers also make nighttime visits to the bathroom more bearable, since the light can be turned down below the blinding level. Be sure to install a switch by each doorway so no one will have to cross the bathroom in the dark.

Storage

In bathrooms, as in kitchens and houses as a whole, it's nearly impossible to include too much storage space. Easy access to grooming supplies and toiletry items is most critical near the sink, tub, shower, and toilet.

Sink Area

The sink includes two primary storage facilities: the vanity and the medicine chest. When selecting a vanity, consider how you will use it. Will it store cleaning supplies? Towels? Underwear? Cosmetics? Hair dryers? All of the above? Your answers to these questions will determine the most efficient combination of cabinet space and drawers. Some stock vanities resemble chests of drawers; others are simple base cabinets; most combine drawer and cabinet space. By elevating the height of the countertop, you can gain additional storage space below.

If you are keeping an existing vanity, you probably can improve its storage capacity by making a few simple modifications. Mount wire racks inside cabinet doors to hold cleaning supplies, a hair dryer, or a curling iron; add shelves or half-shelves to create more space. Take a cue from kitchen cabinetry and include pull-out elements such as a wastebasket, shelves, and towel rods. If budget and space allow, create built-in nooks for stashing your toothbrush, razors, and other grooming aids.

A mirrored medicine chest above the vanity provides ideal storage for cosmetics and toiletries. Choose between surface-mounted and recessed units in a variety of styles. Look for models with adjustable shelves to accommodate items of various sizes, and use cosmetic organizers to keep small items in order. Larger, three-door units provide even more space.

Bathing Area

Look for tub and shower surrounds that have ample built-in niches for storage of shampoos, conditioners, soaps, and bath oils. For more space, buy a rustproof plastic shower caddie. Some versions hang from the showerhead; others attach to shower walls with suction cups.

Use wall space at the ends of the bathtub to mount towel bars. To keep bath salts and lotions handy, place shallow display shelves above the towel bars or on the back wall above the tub. If you have a shower or a tub/shower combination, select doors with towel bars on the outside—an ideal spot for hanging wet towels to dry.

◀ *Shelving units that glide out work better than drawers, because storage items stay neat instead of getting in a jumble.*

➤ This bath built for two is outfitted with compartments so there's no question where items go. The double vanity houses pull-out towel racks, tilt-out drawers, and a trash bin.

Toilet Area

Wall space above a toilet is a fine place to put a wall-mounted cupboard or a freestanding shelf unit that straddles the toilet tank. A low-profile toilet, one with a tank that rises only slightly above seat-level, frees more wall area for storage. This may be an especially attractive option when the wall behind the toilet contains a window.

Other Storage Tips

▪ Use wall space wisely. Hang towel bars above one another. Cap a row of robe hooks or pegs with a shelf; hang towels on the hooks and stack washcloths on the shelf.

▪ Add shelves wherever practical. This could be almost anywhere in the bathroom, since many shelving products come in a variety of widths and can be cut to any length. Corner shelves take advantage of frequently wasted space. Create an illusion of spaciousness (and more storage space) with glass or mirrored shelves.

▪ Revamp an existing closet by converting the bottom half into a chest of drawers or a built-in laundry hamper. Install open shelves or cubicles for rolled bath towels in the upper portion.

▪ Bring in items from other rooms. Chests of drawers, china cabinets, and antique kitchen cupboards add character and storage space. Just remember to finish wood furniture with a moisture-resistant sealer to prevent warping.

▲ Framed with moldings that match the door, this built-in storage unit was carved from space often overlooked in baths—the area between the end of the tub and the wall.

Elements of Good Design 41

Safety

According to American Safety Council statistics, bathrooms are among the most dangerous rooms in the house. Most bathroom accidents involve slips and falls. You'll reduce the risk by keeping a few ideas in mind as you design your bathroom.

Add a Separate Shower

Most accidents occur when people are climbing in and out of a bathtub. If you can do with a shower instead of a tub (or if you have enough room for a separate tub and shower), a walk-in shower without a threshold will reduce the risk of falling. To make your shower safer, equip it with grab bars, a bench, and storage alcoves that eliminate the need to reach far or stoop. Shower doors should be made of laminated glass with a plastic interlayer; tempered glass; or an approved, shatter-resistant plastic. No lighting fixtures, electrical outlets, or switches should be within reach of a person standing or sitting in a tub or shower.

Consider Water Control Height

In a shower-tub combination, mount the faucets 30 to 34 inches above the bottom of the tub so you can reach them from a seated or standing position. For showers, mount faucets 48 to 52 inches from the shower floor. Place showerheads 69 to 72 inches from the bottom of the shower.

Eliminate Steps

Although steps leading to a whirlpool bath or sunken shower look dramatic, they can cause a fall. If steps are necessary, equip them with handrails and a slip-resistant surface. Steps with risers measuring 7 inches or less and treads at least 11 inches deep are the safest size.

Choose Slip-Resistant Flooring

Slip-resistant flooring goes a long way toward making a bathroom safer. Any rug you use should have a rubberized, slip-resistant backing.

Install Grab Bars

Often viewed as a specialized feature of barrier-free bathrooms, grab bars are a sensible addition to any bath. In the shower, for example, a well-placed grab bar greatly reduces risk and enables you to wash between your toes without requiring a tightrope-walker's balancing skills. Install grab bars in the shower, tub, and beside the toilet. Make sure they're properly anchored to framing studs, not just screwed or glued to wallboard.

Avoid Sharp Edges

Another frequent cause of bathroom accidents (often in conjunction with falls) is sharp-edged corners and other sharp protrusions. Choose rounded corners on countertops and other bathroom components. Sharp hooks may pose an impaling risk. Look for rounded, oversize hooks designed especially for bathroom use.

Prevent Burns

If you set the thermostat on your water heater no higher than 120 degrees, your hot water will be plenty warm, yet it won't scald anyone. A pressure-balancing valve will improve matters further by preventing sudden fluctuations in water temperature when someone turns on the dishwasher or flushes a toilet.

Use GFCI Outlets

Install ground-fault circuit interrupters (GFCIs) on all outlets, switches, and light fixtures. These inexpensive devices can prevent electrical shock if installed properly and tested regularly.

Select the Right Hardware

Door hardware that can be unlocked from both sides is the safest for bathrooms. With this kind of lock, you can rescue an incapacitated person or a child who gets locked in.

Hiring a Design Professional

Even if you do come up with a terrific bath plan on your own, it can be a great help to consult a bath designer or architect for advice. By having a professional review your plans, you can avoid costly mistakes and gain fresh perspectives and ideas. Many design professionals are willing to review plans and make suggestions for an hourly consultation fee.

Three types of design professionals offer helpful services for anyone planning a bathroom remodeling project.

■ An architect can oversee engineering and design, including a building's structural, electrical, plumbing, heating, ventilating, air-conditioning, and mechanical systems. Most architects charge $50 to $100 per hour; or, if the project is large, an architect may charge a percentage of the project's overall cost.

■ An interior designer, or a designer who specializes in kitchens and baths, can't help with engineering details, but can help with layout, choice of materials and the way the bath will look and function. Look for certification by the National Kitchen and Bath Association (NKBA).

Evidence of certification means the designer has completed and mastered rigorous instruction, including certified training programs in room layout, storage planning, cabinet installation, plumbing, and lighting.

■ A designer/builder can both design and build the project. Hiring such a firm or individual can help ensure a smooth transition from dreams to reality. Some designer/builders, however, are short on design skills and long on building expertise. Design talent and training don't necessarily come with technical skills.

The scope of your project will help you decide which kind of professional to consult. Small jobs, such as replacing bathroom fixtures, don't require an architect's skills. If your renovation involves remodeling an oddly shaped, cramped, or other geometrically complicated space, however, an architect may be able to advise you better than anyone. No matter what design professional you seek, always ask to see a portfolio of completed projects. This will give you an idea of the kinds and sizes of projects the designer specializes in.

Start a Design Notebook

It's never too early to start collecting visual images that embody aspects of what you want your bathroom to look like. Thumb through magazines and books for ideas. Clip photos that show your favorite design ideas and product possibilities, and put them in a folder. Attend open houses and take notes; visit showrooms and pick up manufacturers' brochures. Put these in your folder, too. Then you'll have plenty of concrete examples to help you communicate your ideas and preferences to your contractor, designer, or both.

From the information you compile, develop three lists. On one, write down all the features you definitely want to include; on the second, note any features you know you don't want; and finally, compile a wish list of items to be included if the space in your home and bathroom and your budget allow.

Do plenty of browsing in hardware stores, home centers, and bathroom-furnishings shops to see what things cost. Remember, you can always pare down your wish list later to fit the budget. Now is the time to dream.

PHASE 2: NARROWING OPTIONS

Making a Plan

It's time to get specific on how to best use the space you need for your bath.

As mentioned in Phase 1, bathroom remodeling projects tend to fall into one of five categories. At the least expensive and least complicated end of the spectrum is the facelift, which involves making cosmetic changes (such as resurfacing walls or replacing fixtures) to an existing bathroom. Somewhat more involved and costly is what we'll call renovating, or changing the layout of fixtures within the existing space, usually in combination with one or more facelifting measures. Next comes expanding an existing bathroom into adjacent space—a closet, hallway, or bedroom, for example. If you need more bathrooms, your options include converting existing square-footage to bathroom use and—at the top end of the cost and complexity scale—building an addition.

It's a rare project that falls neatly into just one of these categories. Most are a blend of strategies. This chapter explores the full range of options, providing examples along the way, to help you develop a remodeling strategy of your own.

➤ *If you have the room and the budget, a large room can be partitioned to form an efficient bath. Here a glass block and tile wall divides the grooming station (with sink) from the shower.*

◄ *A second glass block partition separates the sink area from the tub. All the elements are laid out along one wall.*

Do a Facelift

Small changes can add up to big results. A well-planned facelift will not only bring a fresh, updated look to an older bathroom, it also can make a small bath look and feel more spacious.

Facelifts normally involve paint, wallpaper, countertop-surfacing materials, light fixtures, and accessories. They also can help solve spatial problems. Using space better and making minor adjustments to doors, accessories, and cabinets can improve the way the bathroom functions.

Take a moment to consider what kinds of problems you experience when using the bathroom in question. Just correcting what bothers you can make a big difference and doesn't always require major changes. For example, if the bathroom door bumps into fixtures or blocks cabinets, you might improve matters by changing the direction of the door swing. If you need to keep costs down, don't relocate fixtures, especially the toilet. Sometimes pointing the toilet in a different direction (which can be done without changing any plumbing) can give you more maneuvering room. Or, angle the vanity into a corner. If there's a severe space shortage, install a smaller vanity—or a pedestal sink—and a lower-profile toilet.

When you do a bathroom facelift, reevaluate your bath's storage potential. If the room is more than 5 feet wide, you may have room to add a cabinet or shelves at the foot of the tub. Shelves above the toilet or on the back of the entry door also add storage. (For tips on how to store more, see pages 40 and 41.)

Make a Small Bath Feel Big

You don't have to add square footage to an existing bathroom to make the space work better and seem larger. Just keep the following ideas and areas of improvement in mind. Some fall into the facelift category; others require more extensive remodeling strategies.

■ **Light.** Install adequate lighting to eliminate shadowy corners. Create an illusion of height by focusing low-wattage indirect lighting on the ceiling.

■ **Downsize.** Trade large fixtures for smaller ones. Switch a tub for a corner shower or a bulky vanity for a sleek pedestal sink.

■ **Design.** Use no more than two dominant horizontal lines. The top of wainscoting, for instance, establishes one line. Aligning tops of doors, windows, mirrors, and tub/shower enclosures establishes the second line.

■ **Minimize.** Don't mix a lot of materials: Stick with one, such as tile for floors, walls, and countertops. Get rid of any clutter. Keep wallpaper patterns light and small in scale. Stay away from frilly curtains and furry mats.

■ **Reflect.** Use large mirrors to make walls look like windows.

Resurface the Bathtub

Pedestrian as it may seem, resurfacing an old tub can go a long way toward brightening a tired bathroom. A new coat of epoxy paint can cover up an unsightly color or chipped finish without the mess and expense of replacing the whole fixture. It's a job for professionals but can be done without moving the tub. The procedure takes four to six hours, then the new finish should cure for a few days before the tub is used. It costs between $250 and $400 to repair, refinish, and polish an old tub; a sink can be refinished for about $175. For $5 to $8 per square foot, the same procedure will put a new, gleaming surface on old ceramic tiles.

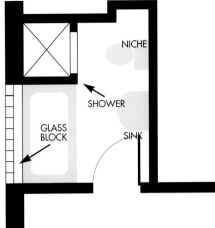

After

▲ *A facelift in this 70-year-old St. Louis home took a 1950s-era bathroom and transformed it into a bath fit for an Italian villa. Before the makeover, the bathroom was structurally sound but lacking in style. All fixtures stayed in their original locations; the sink was replaced.*

➤ *The owners had the old pink and maroon ceramic tile, along with the tub/shower walls and towel bars, reglazed with a white matte epoxy finish. They replaced the deteriorated old subfloor and surfaced it with black and white ceramic tile. Newly painted walls mimic marble, and rich fabrics and vintage laces add to the old-world mood. A new mirror and alabaster marble lights complete the look.*

Making a Plan 47

Renovate

Renovation goes beyond cosmetic changes to encompass replacing fixtures, changing the layout, adding lighting, enlarging or replacing windows, and making any structural changes short of expansion. You'll save money if your plan calls for replacing, rather than moving, the tub, sink, and shower. You'll need to balance your need to move any fixtures against your budget.

Space-Stretching Strategies

As the smallest rooms in most houses, bathrooms pose some of the biggest decorating and remodeling challenges. Tight quarters mean just about every inch must count. Putting one or all of the following ideas into practice will help you end up with a stylish, affordable, hardworking bathroom.

Go for More Counter Space

Forget balancing grooming gear on the edge of a small sink. Augment countertop space by extending the vanity as far as possible on both sides. You'll get even more space if you extend a narrow piece of the countertop over the toilet (remember not to block access to the tank).

◄ *When the owners of this house renovated, they created a vanity and grooming area against one interior wall, tucked the toilet into a small alcove, and set a tub in an unobstructed corner, above. Cabinets were installed to house a media center, strategically located to be viewed while lounging in the tub. They gained the space for the tub by knocking out a wall between the bathroom and the adjacent den (see plans).*

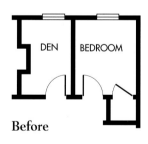

Before

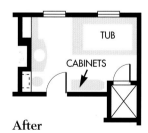

After

Beef Up Storage

Just as older homes never have enough closet space, older bathrooms invariably lack storage. In addition to the other storage ideas in this chapter, replacing a narrow medicine cabinet with a wider one and building cabinetry above the bathtub for seldom-used items are good storage solutions.

Add Light

There's no better way to bring daylight into a bathroom than by adding a skylight, if the bath's location allows it. Be careful—condensation on skylights can cause moisture problems, especially during winter in colder parts of the country. Buy only a high-quality unit and be sure it's installed according to the manufacturer's specifications.

The project requires installing new framing between the bathroom ceiling and the roof to create a skylight shaft. Shafts that flare outward toward the bottom admit more daylight. Paint the shaft white for maximum light transmission and the illusion of more space, or paint it a color to give the bath a glow.

Divide and Conquer

One popular approach to making the most of existing bathroom space is to divide it into compartments. Separating the tub, shower, and toilet from the vanity area with a wall and pocket door creates a division of functions and enhances privacy. This can make it possible for the room to serve more than one user at a time.

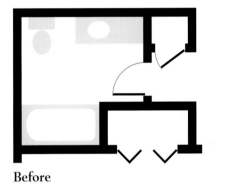

Before

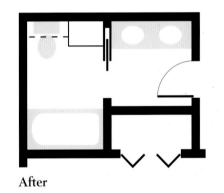

After

▲ By expanding into space formerly occupied by a linen closet, this standard 7×7½-foot bath grew into an efficient, compartmented space. Plans called for removal of the existing sink and relocation of a wall and door. The owners then added an interior wall

with a pocket door that aligns with the existing closet wall at the edge of the tub. To gain more storage, they added a linen cabinet next to the toilet that expands over the fixture, as well as a built-in vanity counter with two sinks by the door.

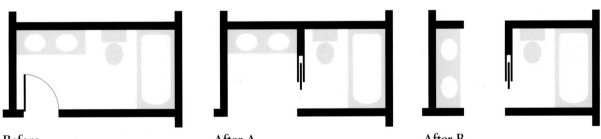

Before   **After A**   **After B**

▲ Before remodeling, this master bath was a single room measuring 5×10½ feet. One way to remodel the bath is shown in After Plan A, where a dividing wall with a pocket door separates the sink area from the toilet and tub area.

After Plan B shows another possible solution. This time the bath is divided into compartments and is accessible from two rooms—an ideal arrangement where a bath adjoins two bedrooms or a bedroom and a walk-in closet.

Make It Snappy

A remodeled bathroom could be the perfect place for design flourishes. Because bathrooms are smaller than most other rooms, the quantities of finish materials required are relatively modest—so you may be able to splurge on extra architectural details and fancier materials without busting your budget. Here are a few design tips to help make your new bath a comfortable, even inspiring, place to be.

■ Gain drama and impact in a modest-size bath with special tile designs.
■ Make views within the room interesting. The least costly way is to use mirrors.
■ Allow subdivided spaces to share light and air. Add an interior window or translucent glazing to walls of compartmented spaces.
■ Don't skimp on windows. Light and ventilation are especially important in bathrooms.

◀ *To stay within a tight budget, the owners of this remodeled bathroom decided against expanding it and employed some design tricks. The room's stylish focal point is the faux-marble mirror pediment created by stacking standard moldings. Perched high and concealing a light fixture, it gives the whole bathroom personality. Opposite this mirror, a matching full-length mirror repeats the design. The owners also made better use of the existing space by swapping the location of the tub, vanity, and toilet and by positioning the door to swing out of, rather than into, the room.*

Expand

If the amount of space in an existing bathroom simply won't do, borrow square footage from adjoining areas. Look first to closets and other spaces that adjoin your current bathroom's "wet wall"—the wall, that is, that already contains plumbing pipes. It's far less expensive to install fixtures when you can connect them to nearby plumbing lines. If you want to expand a master bath, for example, think about keeping the toilet and tub in their original locations and expanding adjacent space to accommodate the sink (or double sinks) and dressing room. That way you save money and labor by not moving the plumbing fixtures that are the most difficult to move.

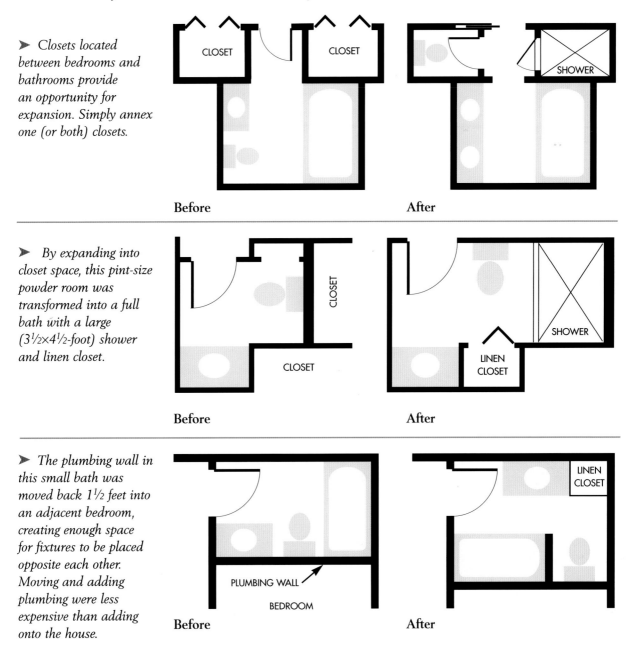

➤ *Closets located between bedrooms and bathrooms provide an opportunity for expansion. Simply annex one (or both) closets.*

Before   **After**

➤ *By expanding into closet space, this pint-size powder room was transformed into a full bath with a large (3½×4½-foot) shower and linen closet.*

Before   **After**

➤ *The plumbing wall in this small bath was moved back 1½ feet into an adjacent bedroom, creating enough space for fixtures to be placed opposite each other. Moving and adding plumbing were less expensive than adding onto the house.*

Before   **After**

Carve Out Space for a New Bath

Facelifting, overhauling, and expanding can do only so much good if what you really need is another bathroom. Before concluding that you need to build an addition to your house, however, examine the existing floor plan. You may find some underused space where a new bathroom would fit in nicely.

But where should you look? Often, a half bath near the family room can take the burden off a one-bath house, as can a secondary bath with a shower stall in the basement. Basement laundry areas are good candidates for conversion because they're already equipped with plumbing. Look,

▲ *This full bath was added in a small attic dormer of a house built in the 1920s. Because the original attic joists weren't strong enough to support the bathroom floor, new joists were added between the old ones. A compact version of a vaulted ceiling and a pair of skylights across from the vanity make the narrow space feel less cramped. To save space, the narrow vanity has a rounded bump-out in the countertop to accommodate the sink.*

too, at spaces close to the bedrooms. A vacant corner of the master bedroom is a likely spot for an additional bath, provided that the bedroom has one dimension that measures at least 16 feet.

Another possibility is to divide a large existing bath into two smaller bathrooms. Provide access to one from the master bedroom and access to the second from a hallway. Or, transform a small bedroom into a full bath, then (if necessary) add another bedroom in another area of the house, such as the attic or basement.

Putting a bathroom in an existing space doesn't have to be a major project that puts you into debt for decades. You may be able to accomplish the job for as little as $4,000 (depending on where you live) if you're careful, practical, and place new fixtures near existing plumbing vents. The main question is where you'll locate the toilet. If the new fixture cannot easily be plumbed into the existing vent stack, the resulting complications can add thousands of dollars to your remodeling budget. In two-story houses, it's most economical to stack the bathrooms directly on top of each other.

Put ease of access first when locating a new bathroom. Many homeowners fail to consider this and make the mistake of putting it in an out-of-the-way place. Size, too, is extremely important. Fitting all the necessities of a bathroom into too small a space is probably an unwise investment. If you don't have the necessary room, think about adding on.

Minimum Measurements

Most design experts agree that the minimum size for a bathroom with a tub, toilet, and sink is 5×7 feet. If necessary, that can be cut to 4½×6 feet. If a shower stall is substituted for the tub, the minimum room size is 3×7 feet. A powder room with sink and toilet should be at least 3×6 feet or 4½ feet square. (For more information about space requirements of fixtures see "Fixtures," page 92.)

Finding Space for a Full Bath

➤ *In this project, a large master bath was divided into two baths. One opens onto the master bedroom, the other onto a second bedroom.*

➤ *Two back-to-back closets yield enough space for a modest bath with shower and two reduced-size closets.*

➤ *This powder room was transformed into a full bath by relocating the toilet and adding a shower in what used to be closet space.*

➤ *Carving a 5×15-foot section out of one large bedroom created space for an efficient compartmented bath between two bedrooms.*

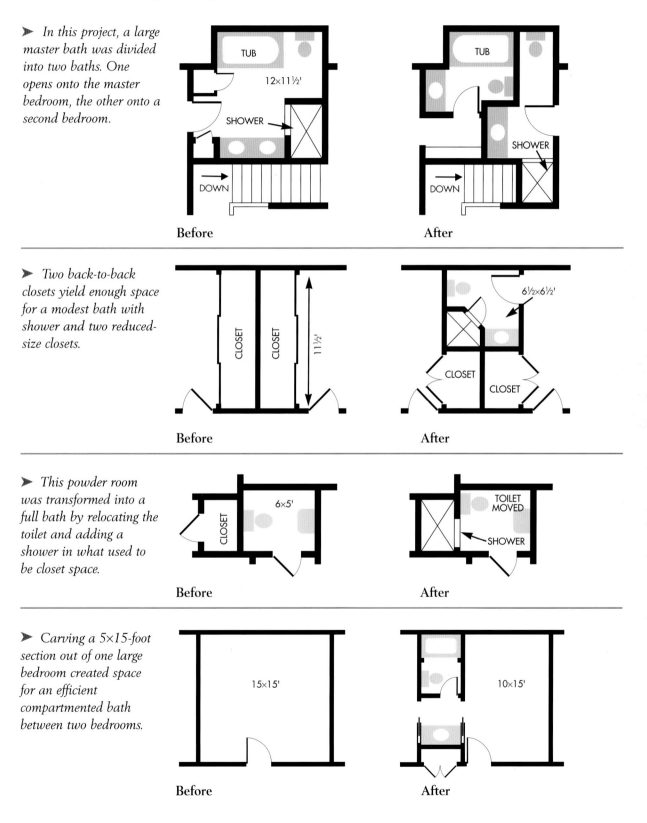

Before

After

Squeeze in a Half Bath

A half bath (or powder room) often can silence morning squabbles over who gets to wash up first. Equipped with a sink and toilet, a half bath can fit into very little space and serve as a small solution to a big problem—especially if you're unable to find enough space for a full bath.

◄ A sliver of space wedged under a stairway provided the ideal spot for this charming 5×6-foot powder room. To enhance the sense of a small, intimate space, wallpaper with a pattern unusually large for the room size envelops the bath. A wallpaper border runs along the ceiling line, mimicking crown molding, and old books nestle in a bookshelf between wall studs. An antique dresser provides a spot for storing hand towels and linens.

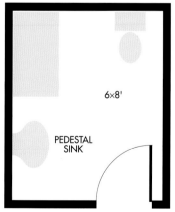

6×8'

PEDESTAL SINK

Good places to consider squeezing in half baths include attics, linen closets, and empty space under stairs. Especially in older houses, nooks can be expanded and hidden spaces opened up. Place a half bath in the most accessible, most functional spot you can find. Use fixtures that are adapted for use in small spaces, if necessary. With a corner-mounted sink and toilet, for example, you can squeeze a powder room into a spot as small as $13\frac{1}{2}$ square feet.

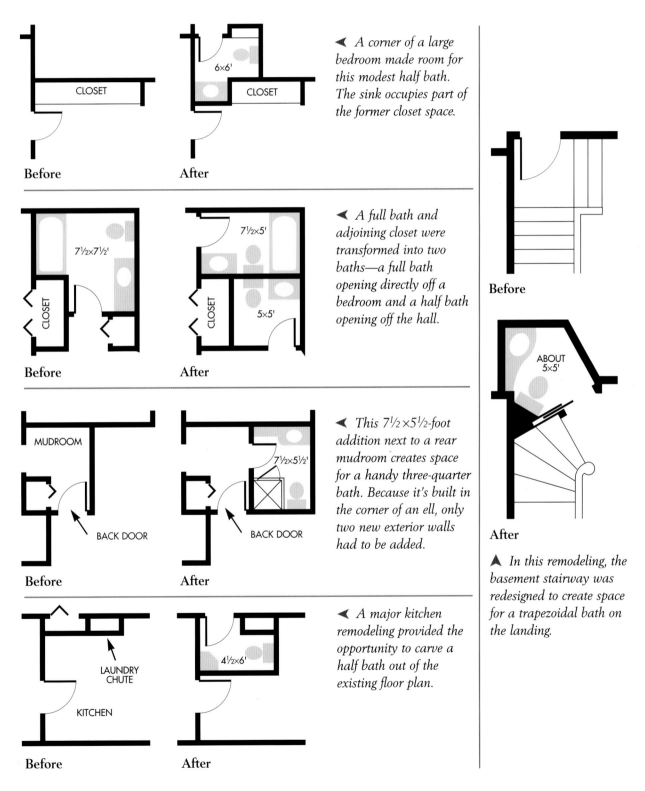

◄ A corner of a large bedroom made room for this modest half bath. The sink occupies part of the former closet space.

◄ A full bath and adjoining closet were transformed into two baths—a full bath opening directly off a bedroom and a half bath opening off the hall.

◄ This $7\frac{1}{2} \times 5\frac{1}{2}$-foot addition next to a rear mudroom creates space for a handy three-quarter bath. Because it's built in the corner of an ell, only two new exterior walls had to be added.

◄ A major kitchen remodeling provided the opportunity to carve a half bath out of the existing floor plan.

▲ In this remodeling, the basement stairway was redesigned to create space for a trapezoidal bath on the landing.

Adding On

Adding a bath to the exterior of the house is generally more expensive than finding room for one inside, but if you don't have space to spare, an addition may be your only choice. Any addition, no matter its future function, can be expensive because it involves laying a foundation.

Bump-outs are a simple extension that can either have their own foundation or be cantilevered—that is, built on top of horizontal beams projecting from the existing structure. Either way, they are short of a full addition and

are therefore less expensive (especially a cantilevered bump-out because no foundation is required). If you build a cantilevered bump-out, be sure to insulate the plumbing in the floor. You'll need at least 8 inches of insulation under the pipes. Check with local building codes.

Even a modest bump-out can yield enough space for a full bath and can provide a good way to expand existing bathrooms to accommodate, for example, a whirlpool bath with windows on three sides, like the bathroom shown *below*.

▲ *Clerestory windows and skylights ensure a flood of sunlight without sacrificing privacy. Mirrors wrap the tub and vanity walls, magnifying light and multiplying space. Radiant heat in the floor and a ceiling fan make the entire space comfortable year-round.*

➤ *On the exterior, matching brick and a harmonizing roof pitch enable the old and new parts of the house to blend inconspicuously.*

◄ *The 6-foot bump-out was all it took to turn an average 8×12-foot bathroom into a spectacular spa. The bump-out made space for a sunny new bathing area with a whirlpool tub angled across one corner and a shower angled across the other.*

Major Additions

If you're designing a bathroom to go in a new addition to your home, here are some preliminary ideas to consider:

▨ Make an accurate "before" drawing of the existing structure, as shown *below left*. Be sure to show your home's exterior features. (See also "Sketch Your Project," pages 60 and 61.)

▨ Choose your location for the bathroom carefully. You'll simplify matters greatly if you choose a location close to existing plumbing. Use an existing window or door opening to provide access to a new bath.

▨ Pick a place where the bath won't be an inappropriate focal point (for example, immediately off the dining room).

▨ The addition will require a foundation if it extends more than 4 feet away from the house. The floor levels and roof of the addition must also tie in structurally with the existing structure (see illustration, *below*).

▨ Follow all relevant plumbing, electrical, and mechanical codes. Also be aware of local zoning ordinances that may restrict how and where you add onto your home.

▨ If your project is more than a bump-out, consider incorporating your new bathroom into an addition with living space. As long as you are incurring the costs of a foundation, exterior walls, and framing, it's often economical to add more square feet than are needed for a bath alone.

▲ *Depending on your property lines, a small addition for a bath can be added to any bedroom. The door to the addition is usually located where there used to be a window.*

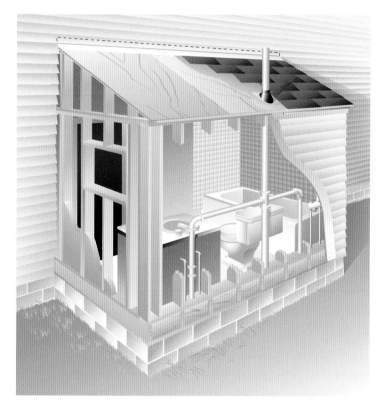

▲ *Part of the expense of a major addition is due to the complexity of the project. Any addition designed to hold a bathroom contains all the elements needed in the main house.*

Seek Advice

For a project as demanding as a room addition, it's wise to enlist the professional services of an architect or qualified bathroom designer, as well as a professional builder. A good designer or design-builder will suggest creative solutions to space problems, ensure that your completed project will meet building codes, and help you avoid costly mistakes. If your remodeling involves structural, electrical, or plumbing changes, local building codes may require you to hire licensed professionals for some of the work.

The bath on this page was professionally designed as part of an addition built onto the second story of a 60-year-old Mission-style house in California. As the floor plan, *below right*, shows, the 900-square-foot addition provides room for an entire master suite, complete with a bath for two, a separate walk-in closet, and a dressing area. The homeowners, who formerly shared a cramped bathroom, now enjoy dual pedestal sinks, a large whirlpool tub, and a roomy shower.

▲ *If your project contains less-common options, such as this large tub that may require additional structural support below, it is wise to consult a design professional.*

▲ *The suite's radiators, salvaged from another vintage building, match those found elsewhere in the home. Between the two sinks, niches in the tile provide storage that often is lost when pedestal sinks are installed.*

Sketch Your Project

It's time to begin planning on paper, whether you're thinking about adding a new bath or updating an old one. Drawing enables you to think visually about your project, will stimulate creativity, and help you identify problems as well as solve them. As you refine your ideas on paper, the drawings will help you communicate your ideas to others should you decide to hire an architect, a bathroom designer, a contractor, or a tradesperson. Or, they'll serve as blueprints if you do the construction work yourself.

You don't have to be a skilled artist or draftsperson to create your own set of plans. The following steps will get you started.

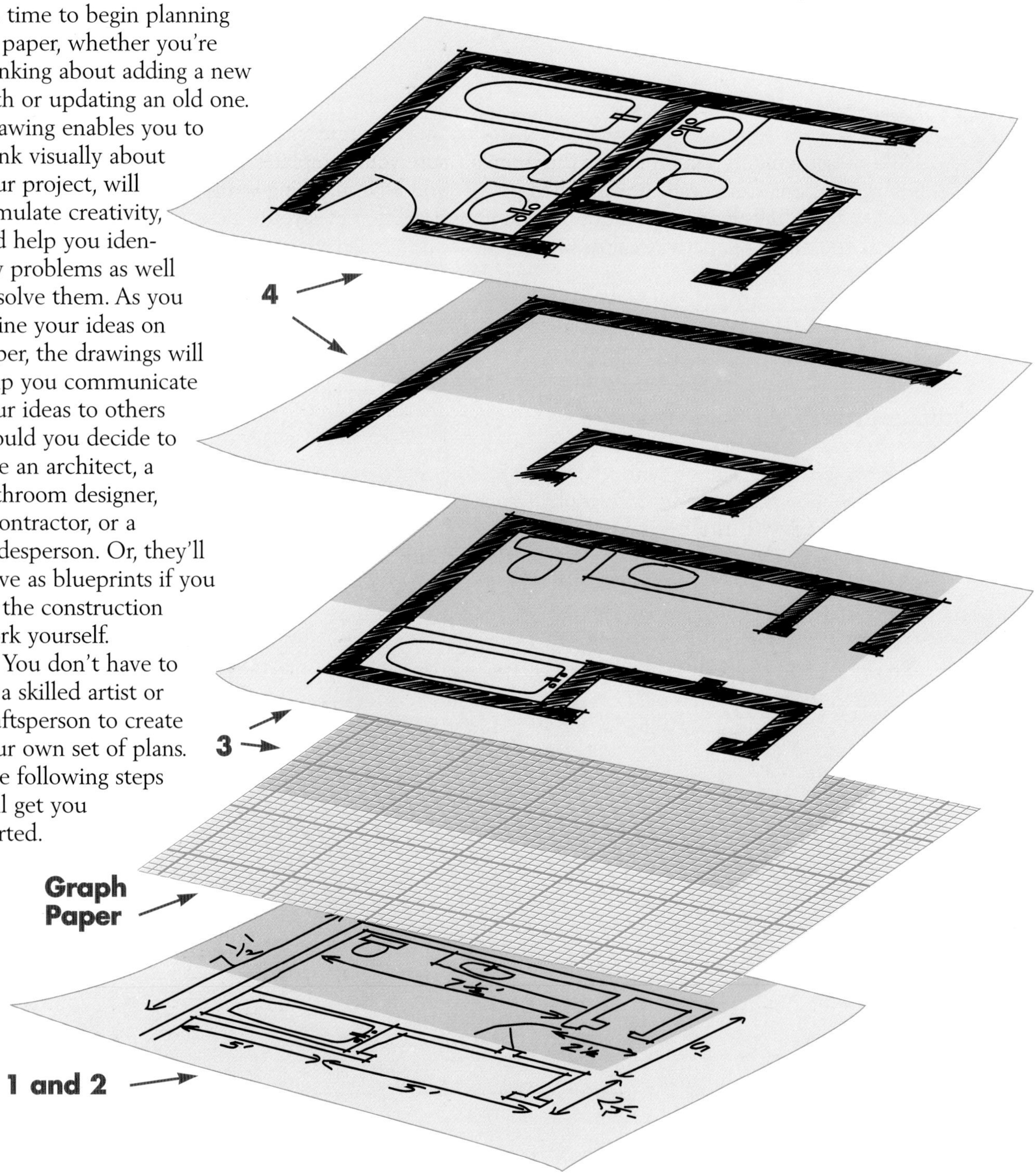

4

3

Graph Paper

1 and 2

1. Make a rough sketch. Begin with a simple freehand sketch of the existing bathroom's floor plan—or, if you are adding a bath, sketch a floor plan of the space as it is now. Don't worry at this point about exact proportions or straight lines. Just draw rough shapes, indicating the locations of doors, windows, air registers, electrical fixtures, and other fixed parts of the room.

2. Add measurements. First measure the room's overall dimensions from wall to wall. Then measure the width of all door and window openings, as well as the distances between openings. Make notes on which way doors swing and add the distances between other fixtures in the room. Write each measurement on your sketch and double-check its accuracy.

In addition to your sketch of the space as it appears from above—called the plan view—draw each wall of the room as though you were looking at it straight on. This horizontal perspective is called the section view. Measure the room's overall height, along with the heights of other fixed features, and record these on your section sketches. If you develop both plan and section drawings of your project, you'll be less likely to overlook something, and every feature of your project can be clearly specified.

3. Convert your rough sketches to scale drawings. Use a scale of ¼-inch equals 1 foot. You'll need a pen or sharp pencil, graph paper with ¼-inch squares, and a good ruler. Masking tape, a clear plastic triangle, an architect's scale, and a T-square also will help. Instead of drawing directly on the graph paper, tape a piece of tracing paper over the graph paper and draw on it (your drawings will be easier to read without extra graph-paper lines to obscure or confuse things). Use the plastic triangle to draw the lines and the T-square to make sure they're parallel.

4. Make scale drawings of the new plan. Using your "before" floor plan drawings as a guide, draw the new bathroom's empty shell on a fresh piece of tracing paper. Fill in only the walls and fixtures

that will remain in the remodeled bathroom. Once you're sure you've drawn everything where it should be, darken the lines and use this as your base drawing. Make it clear on the drawing which walls contain existing plumbing. Tape sheets of tracing paper over this to experiment with new layouts. You may want to make cutout shapes of plumbing fixtures and cabinets so you can move them around with ease. Fixture sizes vary, so be sure your templates correspond with the fixtures you'll be installing in the new bathroom. As you try different layouts, be sure to observe the recommended measurements and minimum clearances described on pages 34 and 35.

Computer-Aided Design

Computers are changing the way bathrooms are designed, both at showrooms and at home. Most home centers and many professional bathroom designers now use special computer programs to translate your ideas and needs into three-dimensional color images of proposed designs. You can see how the different layouts, color choices, and material selections change the way your bathroom will look—before it's even built.

Home computer users can use low-cost software programs to achieve similar effects on their own. Drafting and home-design programs intended for planning whole houses also work for single rooms, including bathrooms. With the right combination of hardware and software, you can dispense with pencils, tracing paper, and T-squares and develop a detailed plan for your remodeling project directly on a computer screen. Then you can print out the drawings.

Case Studies

Capitalize on the experiences gained in these remodeling success stories.

There's no teacher like firsthand experience. Nothing short of your own trials and triumphs can teach you everything you need to know to remodel your particular bathroom, because each project is unique. Being extraordinarily personal spaces, bathrooms come in odd shapes and sizes, and reflect the tastes, needs, and desires of their owners, past and present. Plus, no two houses age in quite the same way—even two identical designs built next door to each other—so you never know for sure what you'll find when you tear down a wall or rip up a floor.

To supplement the general information we've given you, this chapter features a pair of real-life case studies. Two involved homeowners recount their projects, revealing their budgets and passing along insights learned in the course of their labors. Your bathroom plan obviously will differ from theirs, yet these homeowners' stories are bound to help you create the bath you want in the best possible way.

◄ *Before remodeling, this dreary bath was a prime candidate for renovation. A cosmetic makeover done in the mid 1970s had become dated and worn.*

► *The renovation plan called for a complete overhaul with high-quality materials: ceramic tile to replace the old vinyl floor, beaded wainscoting instead of shiny bordello-like wallpaper, and updated fixtures, including a pedestal sink and low-flow toilet.*

Case One:
A Farmhouse Bath Facelift

When Linda Hunter decided to give her bathroom a facelift, she knew what she wanted. The one bathroom in the Midwestern four-square house, where she had lived for 15 years, deserved the farmhouse look characteristic of these American classics built between 1910 and 1920. Though it measured a mere 7×9½ feet, Linda chose not to expand the space, so it retained the home's original character, tiny bath and all.

Linda's budget was flexible: She had $10,000 available but hoped to spend less. She figured she could have the expensive materials she wanted if she saved money by acting as her own general contractor. She hoped this would save about 15 percent of the total cost. Though she had never taken on this responsibility before, she was a veteran of several previous remodeling projects, so she had a good idea of what to expect.

She kept a journal throughout the project. Looking over it now, she marvels at all the important lessons she learned. Here, she distills some of the most memorable ones and describes the steps she followed.

Step One: Establish a Design

I knew that no matter how small the remodeling, priority number one was to get a clear vision of what I wanted. I tried to see the finished project, down to the last detail, in my mind's eye before I began. Then I let that vision guide all my choices—fixtures, flooring, woodwork, paint color, and decor.

I wanted a simple, practical, old-fashioned look modeled after the bathroom in my great-grandmother's farmhouse, a room that exists only in memory, since the old house was torn down years ago. Fortunately, I found a suitable replica in a magazine and clipped out the photo to serve as a guide.

I knew I wanted a pedestal sink and a new low-flow toilet, but I decided to keep the existing square tub-shower fixture. Though a claw-foot tub would have been more authentic, it's difficult to shower in one, and for me having a good shower was important.

In keeping with farmhouse simplicity and to save money, I chose clean, practical porcelain and chrome detailing instead of more expensive gold or brass.

Step Two: Set a Budget

Bathrooms, like kitchens, are expensive rooms to redo. Because my bathroom was small and my tastes relatively simple, I felt confident the project wouldn't cost more than $10,000. I hoped it wouldn't cost more than $7,500. That hazy range became my budget.

Since I took on the task of general contractor to save money, I felt I could splurge on something I badly wanted—synthetic marble (a low-maintenance, long-lasting material) to cover the shower walls. I knew it would be expensive, but I was still shocked to discover its actual cost. The installed cost for 58½ square feet was $2,534, as opposed to $1,100 for ceramic tile (and $4,048 for another more expensive brand of similar material).

Being thrifty by nature, I had a hard time deciding. Finally, though, I convinced myself to spend the money and get the solid-surface marble look-alike. My old house has only one bathroom—why not make it special?

Although I could purchase the synthetic marble for the shower and ceramic tile for the rest of the bath at retail stores, I discovered I would have more styles to choose from if I went through a distributor. The hitch: Only professional contractors and interior designers are allowed to buy through distributors. So, I hired a Certified Bath Designer (CBD) to obtain the product and handle its installation for me. That way, I didn't have to find and hire subcontractors to procure and work with a material I was unfamiliar with.

Step Three: Notify Subcontractors

Next, I made a list of all the subcontractors I'd need to get the job done—a carpenter, plumber, electrician, and painter. I gathered names based on recommendations from friends. Before asking any of the subcontractors for bids, I made sure they did plenty of residential work and wanted me as a customer.

Once I decided which subcontractors to hire, I let them know about when I expected the project to begin. It's best, I learned, to put them on notice early, so they can work you into their schedules. I failed to do this with my plumber, causing headaches and delays when I was knee-deep in construction.

It's a good idea to ask all subcontractors in advance if they can see any problems with your plan. I learned this when, with the old bathroom sink in the trash and a new $500 pedestal sink waiting in the hallway, my plumber took one look at the pipes and shook his head. "It can't be done," he muttered. My heart sank. Turned out he just suffers from terminal negativity, and the job wasn't that difficult after all.

Step Four: Order Materials

Before making a schedule for my project, I made a list and ordered all the materials. And I mean everything. I had to think of every detail—faucets, showerheads, soap dishes, toilet-paper holder, you name it. I learned to allow three to four weeks for shipping and to expect delays.

By ordering all my products before the project began, I wanted to avoid having to purchase something immediately. For me, last-minute purchases made under pressure often turn out to be unwise ones.

When delays occurred, I learned to get on the phone and find out why. The squeaky wheel does indeed get the grease. Become a nuisance, and retailers usually ship your product right away.

➤ *Plastic sheeting covers exposed wallboard before installation of a solid-surface, synthetic marble material. With the tarps, the shower remained usable almost throughout the project.*

Step Five: Schedule Subcontractors

Once all my products arrived, I scheduled the renovation. As mentioned, I discovered too late that I should have paid special attention to when plumbing needed to be done so I could alert the plumber a few days beforehand. You can count on it: If the plumber doesn't arrive at the right time, it will cost dearly in lost time and create scheduling hassles.

Another lesson learned: Expect the renovation to take longer and cost more than you originally calculated. My project took four weeks to complete; I thought it would take 2½. It cost $8,818, a bit beyond my hoped-for $7,500 but well under my $10,000 limit.

Step Six: Enjoy and Appreciate

When the renovation was finally over, the last worker had left, and I had put the final details in place, I made a point of relaxing and enjoying my tailor-made bathroom. A few mistakes were made, but I've learned to live with them gracefully. It's the imperfections that add character, I tell myself. Perhaps someday I'll even learn to love them.

Expert's Insight

(from a general contractor)

■ When a change occurs in your project schedule, call all subcontractors the change will affect and let them know. It takes time, but it's worth the effort. You build goodwill with the subcontractors by letting them know they can count on you.

■ Always check the subcontractors' work, preferably before they've already cleared off the job site. If a subcontractor has done shoddy work, ask (diplomatically but firmly) that it be done over again at no additional charge. Good subcontractors will stand behind the quality of their work.

■ Be available to answer questions throughout the renovation. It may be inconvenient, but you'll be glad later that you stayed on the job site while work was in progress.

■ Whenever possible, buy products locally. You'll cultivate goodwill in the community, receive your orders more quickly, and save time and hassle if you need to return products that don't work out.

Budget (1994 dollars)	
Carpenter (including labor and lumber)	$2,000
Plumber	$496
Electrician (including exhaust fan)	$425
Painter	$713
Bath designer	$1,066
Synthetic marble, installed	$2,534
Fixtures (including faucets, pedestal sink, and toilet)	$1,324
Accessories	$260
TOTAL	$8,818

▲ *After the facelift, this farmhouse bath is clean, bright, and uncluttered. When it's time for a new look, only the wall color needs to be changed, since the background hues are classic and neutral.*

Case Two:
A Do-It-Yourself Redo

For Susan Raibikis, the sweetest sound she'd heard in a long time was the first smack of a sledgehammer when it crashed through her plaster walls. That thud signaled the beginning of the end for a true problem space: a family bathroom with no shower, no storage, and an incurable case of grunge. "The ceiling was so mildewed, people thought I had tried some sort of textured ceiling treatment," Susan says.

What this bath needed was a to-the-studs remodeling. Susan and husband Vic looked long and hard for ways to gain a shower. The problem was that the tub—the logical place to add one—sat under a front window. Vic and Susan eliminated the obvious options one by one. Put a privacy curtain over the window? Too much loss of sunlight. Replace the window with glass block? Unsuitable for the home's style. Expand into a big storage area adjacent to the bathroom? Not in a home of mouse-size closets.

The solution lay in the extra-wide hall outside the bath, which had awkward, built-in cabinetry for linens. By extending the bath 19 inches into the hall space and incorporating the cabinet area, Vic and Susan felt sure they could eke out enough room for a shower. The scheme was appealingly economical. It required only minimal framing work and no relocation of the fixtures. For a second opinion, they called a designer who had helped them with a kitchen remodeling. After reviewing their ideas, she gave the thumbs up, so the plan was set.

➤ *Crisp colors and new lights set off a dollar-stretching overhaul by do-it-yourselfers Susan and Vic Raibikis. They made a small budget go a long way: Sweat equity helped, but the real secret was a smart plan based on borrowed space and simple materials. When the dust cleared, the couple had a fresh, comfortable bath, a new walk-in shower—and change in their pockets.*

Diary of a Remodeling Project

What is it like to live through a five-month bathroom remodeling project while doing most of the work yourself? Susan's journal records some of their highs and lows.

April 11

Time to begin: I guess we've procrastinated long enough. We need to finish this project before beautiful weather makes indoor labor unbearable. Somehow I find myself pouring over pictures from our kitchen remodeling two years ago.

Am I trying to convince myself that we have the ability to undertake this project? Or am I attempting to remind myself of the cost, the disruption, and the mess so I'm better prepared to face another remodeling project?

Unlike the kitchen, which we planned in detail before demolition started, we won't be sure about every part of the bathroom design until the 2×4s within the walls are exposed and we can see the underlying structure. Therefore, we can't outline a daily flowchart of activities or order all the materials. All in good time.

▲ A wooden chute was built to make removing old materials easy and keep the rest of the house cleaner and more livable during the project.

▲ Dust can be one of the biggest hassles of any remodeling project. Hang plastic sheets to block off the contruction area and keep dust at a minimum in the rest of the house. During their remodeling project, Susan and Vic Raibikis went so far as to keep the plastic in place and hand tools to each other underneath the plastic only as they were needed.

April 15

This week has been a whirlwind of activity in preparation for demolition to start. Even though we're not sure what we'll find under the walls, I've been compiling a list of things to do and to purchase as best I can.

We'll build a chute out of scrap lumber. We can park the pickup in the driveway and extend the chute from the bathroom window into the pickup bed. This will eliminate the need (and expense) for a Dumpster.

We've set up a shower in the basement by stapling old shower curtains to the rafters. We'll use the first-floor half bath as our main bath.

April 16

It was a relief when Vic took the first swing with the sledgehammer today. Now there's no turning back. His brother Hank arrived bright and early. Thankfully, he has done a fair amount of remodeling and knows what to expect: MESS! Tarps are hanging in the hall; duct tape covers every crease and crevice in an attempt to keep dust confined.

The walls came down as we thought. However, taking out the tile floor produced our first unexpected hurdle. In 1928, when masons installed the tile, they poured roughly 6 inches of concrete, then individually set the mosaic tiles. Using a sledgehammer to break up the floor might also break up the ceiling in the floor below.

Hank came to the rescue by prying up chunks of the floor with an old Model-T axle. As the dust settles, I'm a bit overwhelmed by the job ahead.

April 17

Moving the hall wall 19 inches presents challenges we don't feel we have the knowledge or experience to handle. We have hired a builder with many years' experience, and I must say it's a relief having this help. This wall supports the roof peak. The builder definitely doesn't require the extra time Vic would have needed.

Before

After

▲ *Family members can now easily deliver dirty clothes to the wicker hamper in the closet via a short laundry chute between the bath and closet.*

April 18

Our new bath is framed in. Unexpected hurdle number two presents itself: the shower. We were going to use a Swanstone [solid-surface] panel kit. We find, however, that we would need to buy a whole extra panel just to cut a piece for a 6-inch stub wall.

I'd love to have a tile shower, but I've never installed tile. Time to get out the how-to books.

April 23

Vic has been running electrical lines and working on the plumbing. It has to be done right, so this part of the project is progressing slowly.

April 25

With the ceiling open and the attic exposed, we had our first visitor last night—a bat. I should have known this would happen.

May 9

Drywalling is a miserable job. The weather has been beautiful, which makes it even easier to postpone work. I have a feeling this project is going to take much longer than expected. As I look at our calendar, I see only two weekends until August 27 when nothing is planned. This project is important, but we don't want it to run our lives.

June 18

All the angles in the ceiling are taking their toll. There are lots of cuts to make in the drywall, and taping and mudding are involved. It takes so many coats of mud.

July 6

I'm putting many miles on my car shopping for materials—vanity, tile, shower door, etc. Since I already have the wallpaper and fabric, I know the look I want to achieve—French country, very crisp and bright.

Before

I have decided to attempt the tile installation in the shower. I've spoken to many people—experts and do-it-yourselfers. After all the work we've done, I'm told the tiling will be a snap.

August 13, 10 a.m.

Our luck—the emerald green dotted tile is on back order. We do have the other two tile patterns we need. I've decided to start with the tub. It should be fairly easy.

Tile Tips

Tile tips Susan collected in the course of her research and labor:

■ Lay out the job with dry tile so as not to end in a corner with a thin sliver of tile.

■ Use a good adhesive intended for bathroom use. Wiggle the tile when you place it on the wall so the tile is firmly imbedded in the adhesive.

■ Use a level to check frequently for straightness, especially in larger areas.

After

▲ *Borrowing space from the hall made room, just barely, for a 36-inch-wide shower and a vanity of the same width. It also left the bath with some tricky ceiling angles that turned drywall work into a jigsaw-puzzle exercise, the worst part of the job.*

August 13, Noon

Piece of cake. I still haven't applied the grout, but putting up the tile was easy. Cutting the tile was the most difficult part. Many cracked, and I really had to be careful with the rope-patterned tile. It is so important to keep checking with the level.

August 13, 4 p.m.

Done with the shower walls. Not too tough.

August 15

The vanity and sink top are in. Major problem. The vanity top we ordered appears off-white on top of the white vanity. It looks horrible. The supplier will take back the top, and we've ordered from a different manufacturer. I assumed white was white.

August 19

The bathtub was refinished today. It looks as good as new.

August 21

The green floor dot tiles still haven't come in. This holds up many other steps. We can't set the toilet or install the vanity. Nor can I give the kids a bath until the floor is complete.

September 6

The dots arrived before Labor Day. Vic had an entire three days alone to finish a lot of work. The floor looks great. We have a working bath! Now on to the decorating.

One problem. Vic dropped a crowbar in the tub. Several chips in the new finish. Ugh. We'll retouch later.

September 28

A beautiful new bathroom. But I will never do another project over the summer—outdoor activities are too tempting. I'm so proud of our home. There's definitely an added satisfaction in having done the bathroom work ourselves.

Budget (1994 dollars)	
Lumber	$ 475
Drywall and cement board	$ 100
Tile	$ 475
Vanity/sink top	$ 395
Toilet	$ 75
Shower pan and door	$ 275
Faucets	$ 275
Lights and towel bars	$ 76
Paint	$ 60
Plumbing and electrical supplies	$ 175
Tub refinishing	$ 225
Wallpaper	$ 105
Labor to relocate wall	$ 300
TOTAL	$3,011

Keep a Journal

Keep a daily journal of stores you've visited, phone calls you've made, names of people you've talked to, model numbers of products you've ordered, and more personal notes about the process. This information may become indispensable during the project when suppliers say they've never heard your name before, even though you've waited six weeks for them to deliver the right faucets. Your journal will prove valuable after the project is over, too, by preserving important financial information, contacts, dates, and lessons learned. Who knows when you'll need to put this knowledge into action again?

The form opposite will provide you with a journal template. Make enough copies of the form to last throughout the days of your project—both during the planning stage and the actual construction.

Create a standard journal page with the following entries, make copies, then keep track of your progress throughout the project.

Remodeling Journal

Page #:   Date:

Contact Person: Phone/Address:

Topic Discussed: Decision:

To Do:

Deliveries:

Notes:

It is permissible to photocopy this page for personal, nonprofit use.

Budgeting

You may have to revise your design and budget many times until they fit realistically with each other.

At this stage, the design for your bathroom remodeling project is emerging with increasing clarity. Now it's time to ask yourself, "Is my dream bath attainable on my budget?"

To answer this question, first you have to establish a budget. You probably already know if you're in the right ballpark. A budget of, say, $1,000 may be realistic if you're refurbishing a powder room with new paint, wallpaper, accessories, and perhaps a water-saving toilet. It's a fantasy budget, however, if your goal is to bump out a wall of your house and create a luxurious master bath.

When reconciling dreams with reality, keep in mind that remodeling is a wonderfully flexible enterprise. All-or-nothing choices are rare, dilemmas and trade-offs common. If you've always wanted a black-and-white tile floor, for example, spend the money for it or you won't be happy with the finished project. Cut corners somewhere else to offset the expense.

If recouping your costs on resale is important to you, beware of overimprovement. Understand the real estate market in your neighborhood and don't spend an amount that would require you to price your house above the going rate for similar properties.

Above all, get informed about how much items and labor cost. With a budget-smart design approach, you may surprise yourself and others at how much style and comfort your money can buy.

> ➤ *Tucked in an attic alcove, this tiny treetop bath was remodeled on a shoestring budget. Because privacy isn't an issue, the window treatment is a simple swag made from a satin-stripe sheet stretched between two cup hooks and knotted. The painted wall treatment combines sponging and stenciling. Only a few new elements were added, including a pedestal sink, beveled mirror, and an easy-to-install glass shelf with porcelain brackets.*

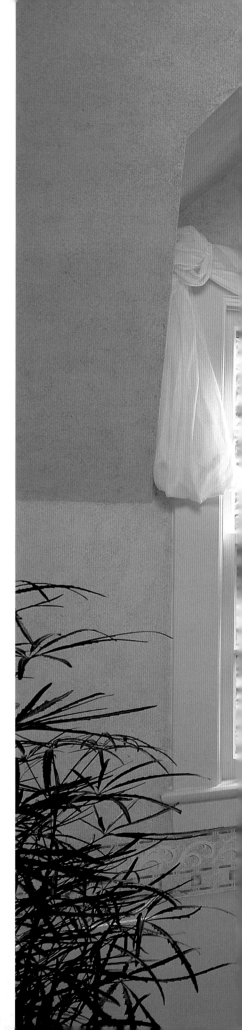

Estimating Costs

You can get a general estimate on the cost of your project in various ways. Talking to contractors and designers is perhaps the best way because their prices reflect local rates. Another is to refer to one of the several books published about construction cost-estimating. *Interior Home Improvement Costs*, published by the R.S. Means Company and revised often, is one such book. These books provide cost estimates for the most popular remodeling projects, including bathroom additions and renovations. Their only drawback is that costs are usually national averages so they may not reflect prices in your area.

Breaking Down the Costs

To arrive at an accurate estimate of how much your project will cost, you'll need to break the job down into all its parts. Go so far as to list each individual component (every plumbing fixture, for example), and plug in the most up-to-date and reliable cost information you can find. The worksheet on pages 80 and 81 will help you do this. Add a 10 to 15 percent "surprise" margin into your remodeling budget to help cover unexpected expenses. The table of costs, *opposite,* shows expenses for the bath, *below.*

◄ *Although you may not be able to draw your planned project this well, it's a good idea to visualize your bathroom to make sure you include all fixtures and materials in your cost estimate. The table,* opposite, *shows the costs for this bathroom.*

Full Bath

Project Size: 7×8 feet

Description	Labor in Hours	Quantity/ Unit	Cost of Materials
Partition wall between vanity and tub: 2×4 plates and studs, 16 inches on center, 8 feet high	0.9	64 L.F.	$31
Drywall: ½ inch thick, water-resistant, taped and finished, 4×8' sheets	1.1	64 S.F.	$22
Paint: ceiling, walls, and door (primer)	0.9	230 S.F.	$8
Paint: ceiling, walls, and door (1 coat)	0.9	230 S.F.	$8
Vanity base cabinet: deluxe, 2-door, 30" wide	1.4	31 Ea.	$311
Vanity top: laminated-plastic-covered	0.8	1 Ea.	$48
Vanity sink: with trim, porcelain enamel on cast iron, 18" round, white	3.1	1 Ea.	$207
Fittings for vanity sink	7.0	1 Set	$94
Bathtub: recessed, mat bottom, 5' long, white	3.6	1 Ea.	$390
Fittings for tub and shower	7.7	1 Set	$146
Curtain rod: stainless steel, 5' long, 1" diameter	.6	1 Ea.	$28
Mirror	.3	1 Ea.	$57
Walls for shower enclosure: 4¼×4¼" ceramic tile	5	50 S.F	$180
Flooring: porcelain tile, one color, 8×8" tiles	3.2	36 S.F	$193
Toilet: tank-type, vitreous china, floor-mounted, 1 piece, white	3.9	1 Ea.	$788
Fittings for toilet	5.3	1 Set	$124
Toilet-tissue dispenser: surface mounted, stainless-steel	0.3	1 Ea.	$12
Towel bar: stainless-steel, 30" long	0.4	1 Ea.	$29
Totals	46.4		**$2,676**
Contractor's fee (including materials)			**$6,418**

Adapted with permission from Interior Home Improvement Costs *(R.S. Means Co., 1996)*

Key to abbreviations
L.F.–linear foot S.F.–square foot Ea.–each

A note on labor hours
Time estimates are for professionals. If you're doing some or all of the work yourself and are not familiar with the tools and procedures involved, plan on spending more time than is indicated on the chart.

Remodeling Paybacks

A successful remodeling project will reward you with enhanced livability and beauty. But will it also pay off when you sell your home?

Adding a second full bath to a house that has one or 1½ baths is nearly certain to pay for itself on resale, according to a 1995 study conducted by *Remodeling*, a magazine for remodeling professionals. The study found, too, that second baths generally enhance a home's value more than third baths do. Also, few things will slow the sale of a house more than an unattractive bath.

Remodeling magazine's cost-versus-value survey went into detail on the average cost of some common remodeling projects and what percentage of those costs a homeowner might expect to recover when selling the house. The map, *opposite*, shows returns for remodeling baths in different regions of the United States.

10 EASY WAYS TO CUT COSTS

1. Do as much of the work yourself as you can. Wallpaper stripping, light demolition, and cleaning up after subcontractors all take more elbow grease than skill. There's no sense in paying skilled carpenters their normal hourly rate to push a broom.

2. Instead of using costly marble or stone, choose synthetic materials for floors, countertops, and walls. Today's laminates, vinyl flooring, ceramic tile, and paint techniques can produce rich-looking surfaces, but you don't necessarily have to be rich to buy them.

3. Instead of having cabinets custom-made, find a line of stock cabinets that you like. Lumberyards carry some styles; your contractor or designer can probably give you literature on many more. Adapt prefabricated cabinets to your needs with easy-to-install storage devices such as wire shelves, retractable baskets, hooks, and drawer dividers.

4. Keep fixture and faucet styles simple. Chrome faucets and basic white fixtures are less expensive than the latest shapes and colors, and they won't look out of fashion in a decade. Update your decor periodically with more easily changeable accessories, such as wall coverings and window treatments.

5. Leave fixtures where they are or at least keep them against walls that contain existing pipes and vent stacks.

6. If you want a whirlpool tub, look for models that come in standard tub sizes. You'll save money by replacing the tub you have instead of rearranging the space to fit an oversize tub.

7. Consider hiring a design professional. Despite the additional fees, you may actually save money because professionals can help you avoid costly mistakes and ensure that the job is done efficiently.

8. If you have the time, act as your own general contractor. This can save you a contractor's markup of 10 to 25 percent. Don't undertake the job lightly, however—see "Building" (pages 102 to 111) for details on what's involved.

9. Purchase building materials during the winter, when demand—and prices—often are lower. Also take advantage of clearance sales. (This assumes that you can store all your materials in a secure, sheltered place until they're needed for the project.)

10. Establish your design in detail, and make sure all your materials are available before the first tradespeople arrive. Changes and holdups during construction can escalate costs.

➤ *Costs vary widely from region to region. The estimated cost for a 5×9-foot bathroom remodeling ranges from a low of $6,625 in Columbia, South Carolina, to a high of $11,240 in Westchester, New York. Estimates for cost recovery show even greater disparities, ranging from 47 percent in Cleveland, Ohio, to 144 percent in Charlotte, North Carolina.*

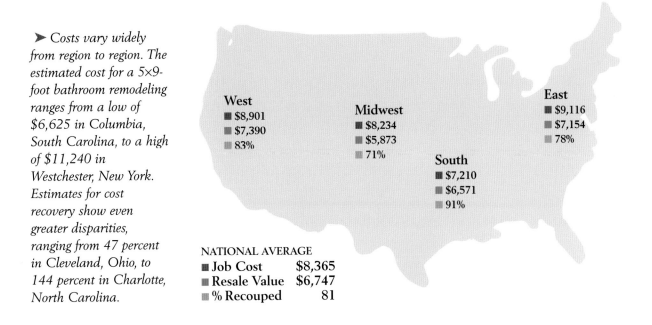

West
- $8,901
- $7,390
- 83%

Midwest
- $8,234
- $5,873
- 71%

East
- $9,116
- $7,154
- 78%

South
- $7,210
- $6,571
- 91%

NATIONAL AVERAGE
- **Job Cost** $8,365
- **Resale Value** $6,747
- **% Recouped**   81

Cost Ranges for Bath Fixtures

As you know, all bathroom fixtures are not created equal. Toilets, for example, range in price from about $50 to more than $500. This chart compares the costs of fixtures in four price/quality categories.

■ Basic prices indicate the least expensive fixtures available at hardware and do-it-yourself discount stores. Standard sizes and colors—white for sinks, tubs, and faucets; chrome for faucets and showerheads—make these items the most affordable.

■ Upgrade prices refer to a wider range of colors and shapes. In some cases, the price increase indicates the use of sturdier finishes or materials—for example, drawers made of wood rather than particleboard.

■ Top-of-the-line prices represent fixtures that have special features, such as colored finishes, shell-shaped basins or ones of other shapes, or one-piece toilet construction.

■ Specialty prices reflect top-quality materials such as marble and gold plating. Items are available in nonstandard sizes and colors, and feature amenities such as heated toilet seats. Specialty items usually are ordered through bathroom showrooms or designers.

	Basic	Upgrade	Top-of-the-Line	Specialty
Vanity sink	$50-150	$125-250	$250-400	$400+
Pedestal sink	$100-225	$200-350	$300-750	$750+
Sink faucets	$50-90	$90-125	$125-500	$500-1,500
Toilet	$50-120	$120-300	$300-600	$600-1,000
Standard tub	$150-200	$200-350	$300-800	$800-4,000
Tub faucets	$75-125	$100-175	$175-500	$500-1,500
Showerheads	$15-50	$30-70	$70-125	$200-400
Shower enclosures	$150-250	$250-400	$475-600	$800-4,000

It's best to break your budget down into its smallest components. We've printed a listing of most of the common items involved in remodeling a bathroom so you can keep track of where you're spending your precious dollars. The column "specification" is used to further define the type of items you're buying right down to their brand names and colors.

Cost Estimates for Bath Remodeling

Description	Specification	Qty.	Cost Per Unit	Cost	Tax	Total Cost	Vendor
Plumbing fixtures							
Vanity sink							
Pedestal sink							
Vanity top							
Sink faucet set							
Bathtub							
Spa-type oval bathtub							
Bathtub faucet/shower set							
Shower stall							
Shower faucet set							
Toilet							
Pipes, straps, vents							
Installation (labor costs)							
Other fixtures							
Shower curtain rod							
Toilet-tissue dispenser							
Towel rods							
Grab bars							
Medicine cabinet with mirror							
Mirror installation							
Shower door							
Shower lining							
Soap dish							
Installation (labor costs)							
Storage							
Cabinets							
Vanity base cabinets							
Mounting screws							
Vanity top							
Medicine cabinet							
Installation (labor costs)							

Description	Specification	Qty.	Cost Per Unit	Cost	Tax	Total Cost	Vendor
Floor							
Plywood underlayment—4'×8'×½"							
Flooring							
Floor felt—500-pound							
Flooring adhesive							
Flooring nails							
Quarter-round trim							
Finishing nails							
Installation (labor costs)							
Tile							
Floor tile							
Wall tile							
Tile—trim							
Grout compound							
Grout sealant							
Tile adhesive							
Soap holder—tile							
Installation (labor costs)							
Lighting and electrical							
Track lights							
Can lights							
Fluorescent fixtures							
Lighting fixtures—sink							
Ground-fault circuit interrupters							
Ventilation exhaust fan							
Heat lamp							
Installation (labor costs)							
Framing							
Lumber							
Nails							
Drywall							
Trim							
Wainscoting							
Installation (labor costs)							
Miscellaneous							

Adapted with permission from The Complete Guide To Being Your Own Remodeling Contractor *by Kent Lester (Betterway Books, Cincinnati, Ohio, 1994).*

Surface Materials

Material choices significantly impact the look and cost of your bath.

A remodeled bath that looks nice but doesn't work from a practical standpoint is bound to disappoint its owners. Assuming that you've designed the room's layout to meet your wishes and needs, the next most important contributor to your long-term happiness with it will be the finish materials— the surfaces, fixtures, and flourishes that both set the style and determine how the room will hold up over time.

Your top priority should be how the materials will function given how you and your family typically will use the bathroom. Beyond that, your best dollar payback will come from equipping your bathroom with materials, fixtures, and features that have become standard in new, comparably priced homes. If you're planning to live in the house for a while, however, make the materials as personal as you please, since resale will be less important than enjoyment value.

This section discusses floors, walls, countertops, and tub/shower enclosures and what materials are available to cover these surfaces. Cost information, how the materials perform, and how they're installed are included. Some materials have more than one application but may function better for one surface than for another.

➤ *A basic white tile bath with little ornamentation can be transformed into a warm room simply by adding colors. Here, bright-colored wainscoting, striped wallpaper, and whimsical soap dishes and holders add sparkle without major changes to the bath's design.*

Floors

Before installing a new floor, check the condition of the subfloor (the material between the floor covering and the floor joists) and the supporting joists. Decayed subflooring, especially around the toilet and tub, is a common problem in older houses. Spot repairs may be adequate, or you may need to replace the entire subfloor. This is an ambitious undertaking, so consult with a professional if you're not sure how to proceed.

Unless you can inspect the underside of the subfloor from the basement, you'll have to pry up a bit of the existing floor covering. Prod around the base of fixtures and cabinets with an awl or screwdriver in search of soft spots.

When choosing floor finishes, remember that your bathroom is the site of daily family traffic and the occasional tub overflow. Remember, too, that slips in the bathroom are a major cause of home accidents. Look for a durable material that is both beautiful and slip-resistant.

Floor Tile

Properly installed, tile is one of the most durable flooring materials. It's the number one choice for bathrooms because it's waterproof, easy to maintain, and stain-resistant. Ceramic tile is available in a wide range of sizes, shapes, and colors, and comes plain or decorated, glazed or matte.

As a bathroom floor covering, however, tile has some drawbacks: It's hard and cool underfoot, and without a textured surface it can be slippery when wet. Tile manufacturers rate tile for slip-resistance on a scale of 1 through 4 (higher numbers indicate better resistance).

The grout that fills the cracks between tiles can be smooth or sandy, white or color-tinted. You can use the grout lines as a design element by choosing a colored grout that contrasts with the tile. Once the grout has set, coat it with a latex sealer to repel moisture.

Ceramic tile costs $12 to $20 per square foot, installed, with the top prices for handmade and hand-painted tile. Standard tile, by itself, sells for around $5 per square foot, then costs an addi-tional $5 to $8 per square foot for installation.

Laying a tile floor can be a good do-it-yourself project, although it requires patience and care. All tile must be installed on a level, clean, unmarred subfloor. Most tile retailers carry the necessary installation supplies and offer instructions for do-it-yourselfers. Always use tiles specifically designed for a floor installation. Tiles manufactured for walls or countertops are not designed to be used as floor tiles.

Warm Floors

Ceramic tile, vinyl, and hardwood floors are popular flooring choices for the bathroom, but they can be bone-chilling in winter. That problem is easily solved with radiant heat panels installed in the floor joists. These operate only when you want them to and can be limited to defined areas, such as in front of the vanity or beside the tub. Look for radiant heat panels in retail building centers and through ceramic tile installers.

Resilient Flooring

This category includes various vinyl and rubber flooring, in sheet and tile form. Resilient flooring is soft underfoot, yet stands up to heavy traffic and resists water penetration. It's available in an array of colors, patterns, and textures. At the bottom end of the price range, vinyl is the least expensive flooring option. High-end vinyl products are comparable in cost to a good carpet or softwood floor.

Vinyl composition tile (combining vinyl resins with filler) costs the least, about $6 per square yard. Rotovinyl (a printed pattern covered by a clear topcoat) costs a bit more. Top-of-the-line inlaid vinyl (vinyl granules are fused together in a solid pattern that goes through to the backing) is the most durable.

Vinyl tiles are sold in 9- and 12-inch-square units that are easy for do-it-yourselfers to handle and cost between $1 and $10 per square foot. Sheet vinyl requires skill to install well and is best left to the pros. Costs range from $5 to $40 per square yard, installed.

Solid rubber tile is another option. Because rubber tile is used mainly in industrial and commercial settings, you may need to work through an interior designer or contractor to get it. Colors are muted and available in a limited range of hues. Installation is tricky so hire professionals. Expect to pay about $40 per square yard.

Resilient flooring can be installed over most other materials if the floor surface is smooth, clean, and solid.

Marble

The costliest of surfacing materials, marble provides a smooth, classic covering for floors. It comes in colors ranging from neutral gray to pastel rose and can have either a polished or satin finish. Although marble is durable, it can be slippery when wet, so think twice before using it in or around showers and tubs.

You can purchase marble in large, thin slabs or in smaller tiles. Slab marble is difficult to install, and its weight may require reinforcing the structure beneath. Check with a professional before choosing marble. Marble tiles are typically ½ inch thick, 8 to 12 inches square, and less costly than the larger slabs. The price of marble varies greatly, and is usually dependent on how far the marble must be shipped, because it is so heavy.

Carpet

While it's comfortable underfoot, carpet has several drawbacks for use in the bathroom. Stains from cleaning products and makeup can be hard or impossible to remove, and poor ventilation in the room can cause moisture to collect and mildew to grow. As a rule, carpets are more practical in dressing and grooming areas of the bathroom than in wet areas.

If you do choose carpeting, look for types that resist mildew, don't retain odors, and are less susceptible to water absorption and staining. Polypropylene carpet doesn't soak up water and is resistant to mold.

Carpeting is easily laid over any existing surface except other carpeting. Carpeting costs from

▲ *A Douglas fir grate, made to fit the floor between tub and shower, allows water to drip through to a drain. The wood adds a warm accent in contrast to the concrete surfaces.*

$16 to $40 per square yard. Use a good, water-resistant pad in any bathroom application. If you have a wooden subfloor and joists below, a water-resistant pad will help protect the wood from the moisture produced in the bathroom.

Wood

Wood floors are common in bathrooms, even though the potential for moisture damage is high. If your heart is set on a wood floor, be sure it's well coated with a urethane finish to protect against moisture penetration. Wood floors generally cost between $5 and $20 a square foot installed and finished. You might consider using one of the newer wood look-alike products made of plastic laminate to achieve the look of wood but the water resistance of a laminate floor. Avoid wood planks that have beveled edges since these form water-collecting grooves on the floor.

Walls

◄ *Meticulously executed details give this bath its stunning appeal. The floor tiles form a perfect grid; the glass partition, tiled wall pattern, and vanity mirror all align at the 8-foot mark establishing a visual line above; and black is used as a dramatic accent on the floor, as cabinet hardware, and for the overhead lighting.*

The quickest way to transform a bath is to change the look of its walls. Whether you choose paint, wallpaper, paneling, or tile, remember that a bathroom wall covering must stand up to heat, moisture, and frequent cleaning. Mixing and matching materials for their strengths in different areas works well, especially if the bathroom is divided into compartments.

Paint

Paint is the least expensive covering for walls and ceilings, and it's the most easily changed for cosmetic makeovers. Besides choosing a color, you'll also need to settle on a finish type, from flat to high-gloss. Gloss and semigloss finishes work best in bathrooms, because they repel water and clean easily. Glossier paints exaggerate all the lumps and bumps on a wall, however, so they must be applied to a flat, smooth surface.

Traditionally, alkyd (oil-based) paints outlasted their latex (water-based) counterparts, but newer latex formulations now rival alkyds for durability. Alkyds dry slowly and require paint thinner instead of soap and water for cleanup. Also, the use of alkyd paints is restricted in some parts of the country because of concerns they damage the environment.

If you want to cover a tile, glass, or porcelain surface, use an epoxy paint. Whichever paint you use, be sure to follow the manufacturer's instructions for preparation and application. Most surfaces must be primed to ensure proper paint adhesion. The majority of any painting job is preparing the surface you plan to paint and masking and draping surfaces you wish to keep free of paint. Though painting walls is an easy do-it-yourself project, you'll need a patient, steady hand (and a good brush) when cutting in around fixtures and cabinets.

Wall Coverings

Wallpaper and vinyl coatings come in many colors, patterns, and textures—some with a prepasted adhesive coating that only needs to be dampened to adhere to the wall. It's best to limit wall coverings to bathroom walls; don't ask for trouble by papering the ceiling of this naturally humid room.

All bath wall coverings should resist moisture and hold up to frequent scrubbing. Ordinary wallpaper is not the answer. Vinyl coverings (particularly vinyl that is laminated to fabric) weather bathroom conditions much better. Products labeled "scrubbable" will tolerate more abrasion than "washable" ones.

Most wall coverings can be applied to a solid, clean surface. Strip or steam off old wallpapers first, and thoroughly wash the stripped walls with a trisodium phosphate cleaner (or a suitable phosphate-free substitute). Some wall coverings require you to size the walls before hanging them. Sizing is the equivalent to priming a wall with paint.

Wood

Wood adds a natural warmth that complements many interior design schemes. As a wall-surfacing material, it comes in the form of premilled solid wood wainscoting or tongue-and-groove beadboard, veneered plywood, or melamine-surfaced hardboard. Both solid wood and plywood-backed veneers must be coated with urethane or another water-resistant coating. Hardboard panels coated with melamine (a thin layer of white plastic) are well suited for baths because melamine is water-resistant and easy to clean.

Ceramic Tile

Ceramic tile is attractive and durable. It won't fade or stain, it cleans easily, and is not merely water resistant but, when installed correctly, fully waterproof. True, ceramic tile is also expensive, but its advantages make it well worth considering for at least some areas in a bathroom.

Like tile intended for floor use, wall tile comes glazed and unglazed, plain and patterned, and in an unlimited palette of colors. In addition to buying stock machine-finished tiles, you can purchase hand-painted tiles or design your own patterns. Wall tiles commonly are 4 or 6 inches square, but many other sizes and shapes are available. Just be sure to use only wall tile for walls and floor tile for floors, since the two are made and finished differently.

You can apply ceramic tile to any drywall, plaster, or plywood surface that's smooth, sound, and firm. Unglazed tile probably will need to be sealed. Installing wall tile is a more difficult do-it-yourself project than laying a tile floor. If you're inexperienced, hire a professional.

Glass Block

Glass block is popular in bathrooms today because of its sleek modern look and its ability to transmit light while preserving privacy. It can be used to create both walls and windows. Glass block is very expensive when compared to other materials you might use. The cost can vary from $40 to $60 per square foot, depending on the complexity of the job, labor costs, and the block you select. It also is a tough job for do-it-yourselfers to do well, even with mortarless "do-it-yourself" systems. For professional results, it's best to call in a mason.

Cabinets

The modest, single-sink vanity has given way to a host of bathroom cabinet and countertop options. Building supply and home centers stock a variety of premade cabinets, including base units, wall units, matching medicine cabinet units, and even floor-to-ceiling storage units. Don't limit yourself to the bathroom department when cabinet-shopping—the kitchen department may have a wider selection, and the differences between kitchen and bath cabinet lines are steadily diminishing.

Like kitchen cabinets, bathroom cabinets are available in two basic styles. American-style cabinets have a face frame made of 1×2 boards applied to the front of the carcasses, with door hinges often visible. European, or frameless, cabinets have no face frame. The doors cover all but a small portion of the cabinet front, and the door hardware is invisible when the doors are closed. Choose standard, face-frame cabinets for a tradi-tional look or frameless units for a sleeker, more contemporary effect.

When shopping for cabinets, look at several brands to get a feel for differences in quality and style. Screws and dowels are a sign of solid con-struction; metal clips or staples suggest inferior quality. Look for tight joints, doors that close solidly, matched grains in wood units, smooth topcoat finishes, and heavy-duty hardware.

The standard width for prefabricated cabinets is 30 inches; they increase in 3- or 6-inch incre-ments. If you can't find exactly what you want in a stock cabinet, a good trim carpenter or cabinet-builder can probably build one for you. Custom cabinetry costs more, but you'll be assured of a snug fit and a style you like.

Cabinets and countertops typically come from separate manufacturers. It's a good idea, however, to buy them from the same supplier to ensure a proper fit.

Countertops

When it comes to countertop materials, look for something that will stand up to water, soap, alcohol- and acetone-based liquids, toothpaste, and cosmetics. Replacing a countertop or adding a new one is a feasible do-it-yourself project, and you don't have to replace the whole cabinet if you don't want to.

Most bathroom countertops are surfaced with one of the following five materials.

Plastic Laminate

At an installed price of $24 to $50 per running foot, plastic laminate offers good value and per-formance. As a result, it is the most widely used countertop material in bathrooms, just as it is in kitchens. Various manufacturers market laminate under different brand names, but they're all basi-cally the same material—a stack of thin plastic layers bonded together under heat and pressure. Laminate countertops clean easily and are resis-tant to water and stains. On the negative side, laminates can burn, wear thin, and dull over time. Hard blows can chip or dent the plastic, and there's no remedy short of replacement.

Available in many colors and patterns, lami-nate finishes range in texture from high-gloss smoothness to a mottled, leatherlike look. Dealers usually have a few standard patterns in stock; you can order others after looking at color chips in the store.

Do-it-yourselfers can buy prefabricated lami-nate vanity tops or have them made to order with a hole for the sink cut where needed. Installing the finished countertop is a fairly easy matter. It is possible to apply pieces of laminate material to an installed particleboard countertop, although a professional will do the job best.

Tile

As it does for floors and walls, ceramic tile makes an attractive, durable finish for countertops. It's available in many colors, designs, and textures. Grout lines that trap dirt and encourage mildew are a drawback, but new grouts and sealers help alleviate these problems. Costs range from $10 to $40 a running foot (as measured from one end of the counter to the other), installed.

Getting professional results with tile is a challenge for do-it-yourselfers. A slightly irregular look can be appropriate for rustic, unglazed quarry tile, but other tile varieties demand greater precision. Using pregrouted tile sheets, or sheets of mosaic tile on a mesh backing, makes it easier to space tiles evenly.

Solid-Surface Material

Solid-surface countertops offer many of the advantages of stone with few of the drawbacks. Cast from an acrylic resin, solid-surface material demands little maintenance and is extremely durable. Intense heat and heavy falling objects (which shouldn't pose much of a threat in bathrooms) can cause damage, but scratches, abrasions, even minor burns can be repaired with fine-grade sandpaper. The methods and tools needed for working with this material are similar to those required for woodworking. However, some manufacturers require that a trained professional install their material.

Solid-surface material is available in white, beige, pastels, and imitation stone. It comes in flat sheets and in ready-formed countertops with integrated sinks. Prices range from about $100 to $250 per running foot, installed.

Wood

As a countertop surface, wood is attractive, versatile, and easy to install. It is, however, especially vulnerable to water damage, and its porosity makes it hard to keep clean. All hardwood and softwood species must be well sealed with polyurethane or marine varnish. Special care should be taken to seal around the edges of

▲ *Solid-surface counters form a smooth, lustrous surface in this modern bath.*

plumbing fixtures so standing water can't seep in and cause wood rot.

Maple butcher block is a popular countertop material in the bath as well as the kitchen. Available in 24-, 30-, and 36-inch widths, butcher block is thicker than standard tops, so to install it you may need to modify plumbing connections. Costs for wood countertops run $25 to $40 per linear foot, installed.

Granite and Marble

Though marble and granite are unrivaled for their beauty, at $125 to $250 a running foot, these classic materials warrant careful thought. Marble stains easily. Granite shrugs off most stains, except from grease (especially if the granite is unsealed). If a solid sheet of stone for your countertop is beyond your budget, granite or marble tiles may be substituted at less cost.

Cultured marble is less expensive and is made from real chips of natural marble embedded in plastic. It's available in sheet form and in standard counter dimensions of 19 and 22 inches deep. Cultured marble comes with or without a wash basin molded into it, for $50 to $80 a running foot, installed. Although easy to clean, cultured marble must be well cared for. Once scratched, it cannot be resurfaced. Follow the manufacturer's recommendations for what type of finish to apply to cultured marble to best protect it.

Tub and Shower Surrounds

Any surface material for a tub or shower surround should be applied on top of water-resistant wall material. The most common type is water-resistant drywall, sometimes called "greenboard" because of its hospital green color. A more durable and water-resistant product is a cement-board product such as Duroc. The cement-board products may be more expensive than greenboard, but the added expense gives you a foundation you know can stand up to the moist environment of the bathroom. The surface material itself must be waterproof, not just water-resistant.

Various manufacturers offer prefabricated surrounds made of fiberglass, acrylic, vinyl, plastic laminate, or synthetic stone. Remodelers should avoid buying a one-piece surround (typically made of molded fiberglass) unless they choose a unit that can be transported into the bathroom through available openings. Multipiece surround kits, which can be assembled inside the bathroom, also are available.

If you decide to create your own bath or tub surround, you have a choice of the following surface materials.

▲ *Although somewhat tricky to install, tile can be placed on many surfaces to visually tie together different elements of a bath.*

Solid-Surface Material

For durable, stylish, easy-to-care-for shower enclosures, solid-surface material is hard to beat. Though sometimes pricey, today's options in this category have a lot to offer. Nothing beats this smooth acrylic surface for ease in cleaning, and the material lasts a lifetime.

For do-it-yourselfers, solid-surface tub and shower kits offer easy installation. These kits generally consist of precut panels and curved corner moldings. They are designed to go with standard fixtures; nonstandard installations require professional help. Prices start at $40 to $75 a square foot installed.

Ceramic Tile

Waterproof, durable, and easy to maintain, ceramic tile is a logical choice for tub and shower surrounds. One drawback: The grout can mildew, making it difficult to clean.

Small mosaic tiles (which measure about 1 inch square) come bonded to sheets of 1×1-foot or 1×2-foot fiber mesh. These sheets go up faster than loose tiles, because you don't have to set each piece individually. Pregrouted sheets of 4-inch-square tiles have flexible synthetic grouting. You stick the sheets to the substrate surface first, then apply a thin bead of caulk around the edges. As with mosaic-tile sheets, installing pregrouted tile sheets is not as time-consuming as laying loose tile nor does it require as much skill.

Fiberglass

Fiberglass is waterproof, durable, and simple to clean. Many companies manufacture three- and five-piece shower/tub surround units in various sizes. Prices start at about $200. Installing these units isn't difficult if your walls are straight and plumb and have been properly prepared. Most kits consist of two molded end panels and one or more center panels.

Bathroom Surface Materials

Floor, wall, and countertop coverings must be moisture-tolerant or they won't stand up well in a bathroom. Look for durable materials that won't trap moisture or mildew and are easily cleaned. With flooring, avoid materials that become slippery when wet. Keep an eye on costs: Finish materials demand a major portion of the budget of a bathroom remodeling project.

Flooring

TYPE	LIFE	MAINTENANCE	COST	RECOMMEND
Hardwood (oak or pine)	Lifetime	Moderate	Moderate	Not highly
Vinyl	20+ years	Easy	Least expensive	Yes
Laminate	10+ years	Easy to moderate	Inexpensive	Yes, but avoid laminates with wood-based cores
Carpet	11 years	High	Moderate	No
Marble	Lifetime	Easy	Very high	Yes
Tile (high-grade installation)	Lifetime	Easy	Moderate (stock) Expensive (designer)	Yes

Wall Covering

TYPE	LIFE	MAINTENANCE	COST	RECOMMEND
Paint	5-10 years	Low	Least expensive	Mildew-resistant
Wallpaper	7 years	Low	Inexpensive	Moisture-resistant
Ceramic tile	Lifetime	Relatively low	Moderate (stock) Expensive (designer)	Highly
Mirrors	Several years	High	Relatively inexpensive	Yes, use acrylic tiles in wet areas
Solid-surface material	Lifetime	Easy	Relatively expensive	Highly

Countertops

TYPE	LIFE	MAINTENANCE	COST	RECOMMEND
Ceramic tile	10-15 years	Moderate	Moderate to high	Yes
Plastic laminate	10-15 years	Easy	Inexpensive	Yes
Marble, granite	20+ years	Easy to moderate	Very expensive	Yes
Solid-surface material	Lifetime	Easy	Expensive	Highly
Wood	20+ years	Can be high	Moderate	Must be treated to resist moisture

Cabinet Costs (Prices are per linear foot)

	Midline Stock	Semicustom*	Top-of-the-line Semicustom*	Carpenter-built Custom
Laminate	$95-190	$130-225	$270-360	$260-570
Veneer	$95-190	N/A	N/A	$360-690
Solid wood	$180-270	$200-360	$360-420	$420-750
Painted wood	$200-360	$225-270	$300-400	$450-930

Semicustom cabinets are built at a cabinetmaker shop to your specifications, not on site.

Fixtures

Choose fixtures by balancing style, function, and cost.

Sinks, tubs, showers, and toilets are the essential components of any bathroom. As such, they need to be durable, practical, and efficient as well as good-looking. Fixtures come in an array of styles, sizes, materials, and colors. Deluxe products such as soaking tubs, programmable showers with multiple heads, foot-massaging whirlpools, and heated compartments for towels and robes bring spalike amenities to the home.

You can boost your bathroom's pamper factor simply by adding an extra towel bar, a shower seat, a heated towel bar, robe hooks, or a supplemental heater. If listening to music or the morning news is integral to your daily routine, install weatherproof stereo speakers right in the shower (although, for safety reasons, controls must remain outside the shower). Add a steam generator and a vapor-proof door, and you have your own steam bath. Home saunas are also available as prefabricated units. They range from small personal saunas up to health-club models that accommodate as many as eight people.

Sometimes, though, the simplest pleasures are the best. A commodious tub, a soothing color scheme, some well-chosen accessories, and a few splashes of bubble bath may be all it takes to turn your bathroom into a palace of sensory delight.

➤ *Standard white fixtures, such as this whirlpool tub and vanity sink, are less expensive than fixtures with color and can be easily spruced up with polished brass faucets and a tile surround and countertop.*

Sinks

Materials

Before you choose a bathroom sink (labeled lavatories by manufacturers), consider how the sink material will influence the way the sink looks, how durable it will be, and how much maintenance it will require. Each of the following materials has its own characteristics.

■ Porcelain-enameled cast iron is extremely durable and is easy to care for, but it's heavy and needs a sturdy support system.

■ Stainless steel is durable and unaffected by household chemicals. The steel, however, tends to collect spots from hard water and soap.

■ Vitreous china has a lustrous surface, is easy to clean, and is the most resistant to discoloration and corrosion. But, it can chip when struck by a heavy object.

■ Fiberglass-reinforced plastic can be molded into novel shapes, but doesn't hold a shine as well as other surfaces and is not as durable as the other materials mentioned.

▲ One of the criticisms of pedestal sinks—that there is nowhere to set items down on them—can be overcome with a larger pedestal sink. This oversize example also provides a focus to this classic bath.

■ Simulated or cultured marble and other solid-surface materials are handsome, but they may chip when struck by a heavy object, and abrasive cleaners may spoil the finish. Shallow nicks and scratches can be removed by sanding gently with fine-grade sandpaper.

Styles

Styles of sinks fall into three categories: those that stand on pedestals, those hung on the wall, and those that rest in vanities.

Pedestal

A pedestal sink not only gives a bathroom distinctive charm, but it also can make a small bathroom look larger because there isn't a wide counter around the sink or storage below the sink itself. These advantages are also the main disadvantages to pedestal sinks since they make for a lack of counter space and less storage.

Wall-Hung

Usually designed for compact spaces, wall-hung sinks have the advantage of squeezing into small spaces. However, like pedestal sinks, wall-hung sinks have no storage below and don't conceal the plumbing below. Wall-hung sinks often are used in baths designed for people with disabilities because they can be installed at any height and have a clear space underneath that allows for wheelchair access.

Vanity

Vanity sinks have lots of countertop space around them and handy storage below. Their main drawback is they require the most floor space of any sink style.

Sinks in vanities can be attached to the vanity in a variety of ways.

■ A self-rimming or surface-mounted sink sits on top of the counter after the sink is dropped into a hole large enough to accommodate the sink bowl but smaller than the outside rim of the sink. The outside rim is a ridge that forms a tight seal with the countertop. These types of sinks are perhaps the easiest to install because the hole in the countertop need not be perfect because it's hidden once the sink is installed.

■ Rimmed sinks sit just slightly above the countertop with a tight-fitting metal rim joining the sink and the countertop. The rim is made with different finishes to match whatever faucet you have. Disadvantages to rim sinks are that the rim joint can be difficult to clean, and they are difficult to install.

■ Undermounted sinks are attached to the bottom of the countertop giving a clean, tailored look. Undermounted sinks, like rimmed sinks, are sometimes difficult to clean where they attach to the counter—in this case, underneath the lip of the counter that hangs over the bowl.

■ Integral sinks are part of the same piece of material as the vanity's counter. Because there is no joint between bowl and countertop, it's easy to clean. The main disadvantage is that the entire unit must be replaced if any part of it is damaged.

Buyer's Guide

■ Sinks can make a stylish statement with bowls that are round, oval, rectangular, or asymmetrical—all available in a rainbow of colors. Some of the more expensive models are adorned with hand-painted designs.

■ Choose the largest sink you can fit into your bath. Larger sinks are more comfortable to use, and they reduce the amount of water that splashes out of the bowl.

■ If you are purchasing all new fixtures for a bath, look for matching sink, toilet, and bathtub combinations.

Faucets

Most bathroom faucets receive heavy daily use, so don't choose one that simply looks good—also consider ease of use, safety, and durability. With faucets, price is a fairly accurate measure of quality. A warranty is a good indication of a higher quality faucet.

The best sets, costing from $250 to $550, are made of brass and come in various finishes and designs. Some brass faucets can contain relatively high levels of lead. If lead in your water is a concern, look for lead-free brass faucets and always allow the faucet to run for a minute before drinking the water. Faucet finishes include chrome, polished brass, colored epoxy coating, pewter, nickel, and gold. Polished brass finishes usually are coated to keep them from tarnishing. Chrome is the standard finish for most faucets because it is durable and cleans up easily.

Make sure the faucet set is the proper size and design to fit your plumbing fixture. Most sinks have holes predrilled in their rims to accommodate standard faucets and plumbing. Faucets come in three standard types: center-set, spread-fit, and single-control. Center-set and spread-fit faucets are similar, since they both have two separate control handles (one for hot water, one for cold water) plus a spout. The difference between them is that center-set faucets are connected above the sink deck and appear to consist of a single unit; spread-set faucets have no visible connection between the controls and the faucet because the valves and mixing chamber connect underneath the sink. Single-control faucets also consist of a single unit but have one central control device (usually a prominent lever or knob) instead of two separate control valves.

Although single-control faucets can be elegant and convenient, they sometimes are trickier to operate with the desired results for sinks, tubs, and showers. Choose them with caution for bathrooms intended for use by either the very old or the very young. To prevent the possibility of hot-water burns, you might want to choose a faucet with a built-in temperature-limiting valve.

Tubs

Before buying a tub, literally try it on for size. Climb in, settle back, and imagine yourself soaking. Does it fit and feel comfortable for you? Don't be embarrassed to do this—it's the best way to determine if you'll be satisfied with it.

For the past 40 years or so, the majority of bathtubs sold were made of enameled steel. These are the familiar, steep-sided units that have one finished side. When installed, they butt up against a back wall and two side walls. Corner tubs, which have one finished end as well as a finished side, come in right-handed or left-handed versions (depending on which end wall the tub is against). Steel is lightweight and inexpensive, but it's cold and slippery, and readily transmits sound.

Enameled cast iron–the classic material of old-fashioned, freestanding tubs—offers the greatest quality with excellent durability and better footing than steel. Cast-iron tubs are extremely heavy, however, and may require beefed-up structural framing so they may cost substantially more to install.

Fiberglass-reinforced acrylic tubs weigh and cost substantially less than cast-iron ones. Acrylic has the added advantage that it can be molded into elaborate, body-hugging shapes with integral armrests, headrests, and recesses for grab bars.

Two disadvantages to the material are that abrasive cleaners will damage the surface and all edges and stress points must be fully supported by the structure below, making tubs made from this material difficult to install.

Marble-composition tubs are composed of 80 percent resin and 20 percent marble and are becoming popular in the high-end market. Not only do they come in every imaginable color and a host of shapes, but they also retain heat well, are lightweight, and are scratch-resistant. The only drawback to tubs made from this material is that it may take longer than usual for delivery.

Standard tub size is 5 feet long and 14 inches deep, although 16-inch-deep models are more comfortable to bathe in. But many other sizes and shapes are available in various materials. Before completing a purchase, take careful measurements of your space to make sure your chosen tub will fit through doorways to the bathroom—with room to install it.

Whirlpools and Soaking Tubs

As with bathtubs, the highest-quality whirlpool and soaking tubs are made from enameled cast iron or marble-composition material. Acrylic models allow for tubs to be molded in a variety of shapes. Standard models are 60 inches long by 30 inches wide. The best hydrojet systems are fully adjustable, allowing changes in the direction of water flow as well as the air-water ratio. Most whirlpool manufacturers offer units that can be dropped into spaces that standard tubs occupy.

The capacity of your water heater is a consideration. Larger whirlpool and soaking tubs hold up to 90 gallons of water. If your water heater can't handle the load—or if your community faces water shortages—perhaps you should choose a smaller tub. Some tubs have heaters built-in, eliminating the need for a larger heater.

➤ *This curvy, elevated whirlpool tub, along with the top-of-the-line ceramic-tile wall covering and tub siding, adds to this bath's sophisticated look.*

Buyer's Guide

■ Among the special features offered in tubs today are multiple jets, as many as 12. Jets come in different types—you can get those that shoot out water and kinds that rotate or fan back and forth, providing bathers with a comfortable massage.

■ For greater comfort while you relax and soak, you can have special pillows designed to be used underwater in your bathtub.

■ Special heaters can be installed in tubs to keep water hot (sometimes necessary if you want to soak for a long time).

Showers

If showering in your bathroom means standing under an anemic dribble while you stare at mildewing grout, it's high time for an update. Today's shower options replace the old drizzle with new sizzle. Products now on the market enable you to immerse yourself under a waterfall, melt away stress with multiple massaging sprays, or wrap up in a relaxing blanket of steam.

Before attempting a shower makeover, however, consult a plumber to determine how much work would be involved and whether your home's water pressure is sufficient to accommodate the water features you desire.

If you do add a shower, you can opt to design a custom-made enclosure with the materials of your choice, or you can buy a prefabricated unit.

Another option that's increasingly popular in high-end baths is to enclose showers with walls and doors made of laminated safety glass.

Prefabricated shower kits come with a base, walls, and door, and are available in a wide range of sizes, styles, colors, and shapes—including rectangular, angled, round, and square. Generally fabricated of molded plastics (such as acrylic or fiberglass), prefab units are also available in solid-surface material, which provides a durable and nearly maintenance-free shower stall.

Custom showers can be framed with stud walls and finished with a variety of materials, such as tile, glass block, solid-surface material, and marble (for more information on materials for shower surrounds, see page 90).

◄ *Although slightly more expensive than other options, glass block can be the ideal material for shower enclosures. It transmits light, making for a safer, well-lit shower, and at the same time provides privacy because it distorts the light that shines through.*

Unless you have an open or half-wall shower, you'll need a curtain or door. Curtains are available in fabric and synthetic materials (polyester and vinyl), which tend to mildew less than natural materials woven into fabrics. Although some vinyl shower curtains may be machine-washable, it's best to regularly wipe the curtain with a plastic cleaner (one without ammonia) or a solution of hot water and white vinegar to keep mildew at bay. Cotton and polyester fabrics can be washed and ironed, but they will lose some of their stiffness and water resistance in the washing machine.

Solid doors start at about $100 for an aluminum-framed Plexiglas unit. Prices range up to more than $4,000 for a door made of hand-etched safety glass with a brass or stainless-steel frame. Choose a solid door that doesn't wobble and stays shut when it's supposed to.

Shower Facts

■ A shower can be as small as 32×32 inches, but a 36×36-inch shower is considered the minimum for comfort and safety; anything smaller limits elbow room and the ability to step out of the stream if water temperature suddenly changes.
■ To make shaving in the shower easier, include a fog-free mirror and a niche (or a shelf that drains) for shaving accessories.
■ For safety, all shelves should be recessed into alcoves. Eliminate as many protrusions as possible in and around showers and tubs so they won't be in the way in case of a fall.

Shower Faucets

Shower faucets should be accessible from outside and inside the shower enclosure so the water flow and temperature can be adjusted from either place. The National Kitchen and Bath Association recommends that shower faucets be offset toward the shower door rather than centered below the showerhead. This makes it easier to control the water flow without getting wet.

Standard shower faucets are available with separate hot and cold controls or with a single-handle control. Spending more for high-quality shower controls will probably pay off in longer, more trouble-free service. A high-quality shower faucet carries a warranty and is made from heavy brass parts that are easy to replace.

Showerheads

Like other bathroom fixtures, a wide variety of showerheads are now available in most hardware stores and home centers. Simple water-saving models are available for less than $5; elaborate models with massage settings and other adjustments can cost $30 or more. Some of the higher-end showerheads can be programmed for water temperature and flow rate.

Hand-held showerheads (often equipped with adjustable-flow heads) allow more freedom for directing the spray. Some hand-held models can be mounted on a vertical bar, allowing the entire spray mechanism to slide up and down. Because they are versatile and adjustable, hand-held showerheads work well for children and disabled people. An alternative to the traditional showerhead is the shower bar, which contains several nozzles arranged in a row.

Nozzle Facts

■ Before federal law changed in 1994, the standard shower faucet had a flow rate of 3.4 gallons a minute. Now manufacturers are required to make shower faucets with maximum flow rates of 2.5 gallons a minute. When buying a showerhead, remember, a bigger head doesn't necessarily give you more flow.
■ Some showerheads save water—and money—with a "pause" setting that interrupts the flow during periods of shaving or lathering up.

Buyer's Guide

For a truly relaxing experience, add a steam generator, which can be purchased as a kit to be retrofitted in an existing shower, or you can buy one as part of a prefabricated shower unit. Be sure your shower has a seat, a ceiling, and a door that seals shut to keep the steam in.

Toilets

▲ *Low-profile toilets take up the same floor space as standard toilets but are less intrusive visually.*

To comply with the Energy Policy Act of 1992, toilets manufactured after January 1, 1994, must use no more than 1.6 gallons of water per flush. New toilets cost more than older models, but because old models use 3.5 or more gallons of water per flush, savings on water and sewer bills soon make up the difference. Low-flow toilets compensate for their reduced water volume by generating greater water velocity when flushing.

Nearly always made of vitreous china, toilets are made in three configurations. Traditional two-piece styles have a separate water tank that fits on top of a commode base, or bowl. They are less expensive than other models but are a little more difficult to install. One-piece, also called low-profile models, have the tank and bowl molded together. One-piece toilets have a quieter flushing sound than other toilets. Elongated toilets have bowls that extend about 2 inches farther in

front than standard models and are available in both one- and two-piece versions. Elongated toilets are generally considered to be more comfortable to sit on.

All the toilets previously listed use the force of gravity to flush. Pressure-assisted models are also available; these boost water velocity with compressed air and use very little water.

Commode Performance

■ One-piece toilets cost more than most two-piece models, but they offer contemporary styling and are a bit easier to clean.

■ Pressure-assisted toilets are the most effective at disposing waste, but they are noisier and more expensive than standard toilets, which operate by using gravity.

■ For the least amount of scrubbing, buy the toilet with the largest horizontal water surface in the bowl.

■ Some toilet tanks are insulated to stop water from condensing on the surface.

■ Some newer toilets are 16 or 17 inches high at the seat level (as opposed to the conventional 14-inch-tall models) and are designed for taller people and those with back problems.

Bidets

Bidets were introduced in France in the early 18th century, and their use spread throughout Europe. Though still somewhat rare in the United States, they are becoming more common in luxury bathrooms. The bidet usually is installed right next to the toilet and comes equipped with spigots that produce a gentle wash for comfort and personal hygiene. To use a bidet, simply sit astride it, facing the faucets. Unlike a toilet, a bidet must be plumbed with both hot and cold water as well as a drain. Most models take up at least 3 square feet of floor space.

Tracking Purchases

As with household appliances, it's a good idea to keep track of your purchases for all your new bathroom fixtures—you may be extremely glad you wrote it down when you need the information later. If you ever have a problem with any of the fixtures you've bought, or need to replace a broken one, you'll know exactly what model you need so you can return your bath to its previous condition.

List all your new fixtures as you purchase them, using the form below. Include brand names, model numbers, and colors. Before ordering, double-check all measurements. Upon delivery, check the products for correct specifications and make sure they are in perfect condition. If your payments will be made in several installments, track each payment by writing it down on the next line.

Purchase Order Log

DATE ORDERED	DESCRIPTION	VENDOR	DATE DELIVERED	PAYMENTS	CHECK NUMBER	AMOUNT	TOTAL PAID

It is permissible to photocopy this page for personal, nonprofit use.

Getting It Done

It's time to turn your plans into a beautiful bath.

With carefully thought-out remodeling plans and specifications in hand, you're heading into the home stretch—and you haven't driven a nail yet or even removed the toothbrushes from their holders. Before you do, read this section. It covers what you'll need to know about the construction process, from finding and scheduling tradespeople to coping with the chaos that comes with every remodeling project.

If you've lived through a remodeling project before, you know something about what to expect. But if this is your first major home improvement effort, be prepared to endure plenty of mess and disruption. The more thorough your planning, the more smoothly the project will probably go. Yet even the best-laid plans can be waylaid by incompetent workers, improperly filled orders for delivered goods, or defective materials. Unanticipated problems with your house—especially if it's older—also could come to light during demolition or construction.

Despite these caveats, it's important to embark upon a construction project with a positive attitude. Expect the best and enjoy the process. A beautiful new bathroom will add significantly to your enjoyment of, and investment in, your home.

➤ *To save time and money during construction, consider buying stock cabinetry rather than having some custom-built. A wide variety of styles of stock cabinetry are available to fit with any bath's look.*

What Kind of Contractor?

Hiring a skilled, dependable contractor is the most important step toward carrying out your remodeling plan in a timely, gratifying, and cost-effective manner. There are several kinds of contractors and subcontractors, however, so you'll want to match your remodeling needs with the scope and capabilities of the people you hire to handle your project. Remodeling workers fall into four general categories.

Repair Workers

Classified-ad sections usually are rife with the names of handy generalists, jack-of-all-trades people who can do a little bit of everything, from demolition and debris-hauling to carpentry, minor plumbing, and painting. Such workers can be just right for small jobs, such as replacing a door, adding a new window, and making repairs. These people usually work alone or with one helper. Many are retirees who just enjoy staying busy. They charge less per hour than specialized tradespeople. Consider hiring one if the job is small. No matter what kind of worker you hire you always should ask for references and spend the time to check them.

Tradespeople

When you have a larger project, but one that involves only a single trade (such as a plumber, electrician, or carpenter), you can save money by hiring these tradespeople yourself. If you want just a new sink, tub, or fiberglass shower unit, for example, hire a reputable plumber. Most will handle the entire job (even if there is a little carpentry involved) themselves.

General Contractors

For projects that require two or more specialized tradespeople, consider hiring a general remodeling contractor. This person or company will manage the entire project from start to finish. You'll get a single bid, and you won't have to worry about hiring and scheduling all the required subcontractors. Your overall costs will be somewhat higher, because you'll pay something for the contractor's labor and overhead in addition to the subcontractors' labor costs. But if the contractor is good, you will save time, headaches, and glitches that could arise from coordinating product deliveries and tradespeople.

Design/Building Firms

This is an increasingly popular type of building and remodeling contractor who offers design services along with general contracting services. Most of these firms charge an initial fee (from $50 to $150 and up, depending on the project's complexity) for drawings and estimates. The advantage of going this route is that you eliminate any possible conflicts or misunderstandings between an architect or residential designer and your builder. Plus, you can see what your project will look like before it's too late to make changes. If you plan to build an addition or to substantially alter your home—and you don't plan to hire an architect—consider a design/building contractor.

Hiring a Contractor

Finding a good contractor and establishing an effective working relationship can be difficult but is integral to a smooth remodeling project. The following tips will help you choose wisely.

■ Get the names of several contractors. Ask for recommendations from your architect or designer, friends and neighbors, colleagues at work, a home improvement loan officer at a local bank, or even a trusted employee of a nearby hardware store or home improvement center.

■ Get rough estimates from any and all contractors who interest you. A rough estimate isn't as precise as a bid, but going through this stage with several contractors will give you some idea of how candid and straightforward they are when the subject turns to money.

■ Before you call any contractors back to ask for final bids, obtain references and check them thoroughly. Talk again with the people who recommended the contractors. Ask yourself and others: Have these contractors proved themselves competent to complete projects of the same scale as yours? Check with your local Better Business Bureau office to see if complaints have been made about any of your finalists. Narrow down your list of candidates to no more than five and no fewer than three.

■ Get at least three bids. Ask to have the bids by a certain date, allowing the contractors about three weeks. Review the bids. Some may be more inclusive than others, so make sure you're comparing apples with apples. Good contractors use top-grade materials and hire skilled subcontractors; this will be reflected in their bids. Regard a bid that comes in much lower than the others with healthy skepticism.

■ Don't base your decision on the bid alone. Remodeling a bathroom you will enjoy for years requires that you have a good working relationship with your contractor.

■ Don't make the last payment to your contractor until (1) you're satisfied all subcontractors and suppliers have been paid (ask to see written proof); (2) the job has passed building inspection; and (3) you and the contractor walk through the project and agree that the job is complete.

Questions to Ask Before the Bid

Your prebid meetings with potential contractors constitute some of the most important time you'll spend on the remodeling process. You'll get a first impression of how much you like and trust each contractor. They'll have the opportunity to offer you their ideas about your project, to explore potential improvements or changes to your plan, and to discuss materials and products to be used.

To get an accurate bid, you and the contractor need to communicate clearly. Don't hesitate to ask tough questions, such as:

■ "Where is your office?" An office address can indicate stability and size or be a warning. Many rip-off artists have home addresses, and you should be suspicious of post-office boxes. However, a home address doesn't mean a person is dishonest; many great craftspeople base their businesses in their homes or garages.

■ "How long have you been in business?" Simply put, the longer the better.

■ "Who is your banker?" Find out who finances the contractor's company and contact this credit provider. Ask about the company's solvency. You don't want your contractor to go bankrupt in the middle of your project.

■ "Do you carry insurance?" No insurance, no deal. Make that a firm rule. Otherwise, you will be liable for all accidents that occur on your property. Most contractors carry a card or certificate of insurance. Ask to see it. Every contractor's insurance should, at a minimum, cover property damage, liability, and workers' compensation.

The Bidding Process

■ Be candid with the contractors who will be preparing bids for you. Let them know you have a budget and intend to stick with it. At the same time, let them know you are realistic about what it will take to see your plans through to a successful completion.

■ Give each contractor a set of drawings and a complete materials list. The more complete the drawings, the more accurate and consistent the bids will be, and the easier they'll be to compare.

■ Your blueprints and materials list should specify the quantity of materials you want, plus the brand names, patterns, and model numbers of fix-tures and finish materials. Each contractor should give you only one price: the total out-of-pocket costs to you, including labor, materials, subcontractors, taxes, and fees.

■ When comparing bids, lay aside any that are much higher or much lower than the rest. Concentrate on those proposals that fall within 15 to 20 percent of each other. If all the bids vary widely, probe the contractors for the reason. You may discover the bids don't all cover the same items. In that case, provide each contractor with more specific information about the project to ensure an accurate comparison.

The Contract

Once you've chosen a bid, you'll need to negotiate a contract. Each remodeling company or contractor may have a preferred contract form. All of these forms are not alike, but a good contract should at least contain the following elements.

■ Description of work. This portion of the contract includes all the work to be done (including subcontracting) and specifies materials and surface finishes. A good contract also addresses sticky points—such as weather-related delays or change orders—so everyone knows how they will be handled.

■ Price. Fixed-price contracts should specify the total cost of the job. Cost-plus contracts should specify the cost of materials, the basic labor costs, plus the rates for additional labor.

■ Pay schedule. This part of the contract spells out when you pay the contractor. Many contracts provide for payment in two installments—one in the middle of the project and one at the end. Some contractors may require a good faith or earnest money payment before work begins. State laws may limit such up-front payments.

■ Approximate calendar dates for start and finish of work. Build in some flexibility for delays due to weather or back orders of scarce products.

■ Right of recision. This provision gives the homeowner the right to back out of the contract within 72 hours of signing.

■ Certificate of insurance. This section guarantees that the contractor has appropriate insurance and names the insurance agent.

■ Warranty. Look for a guarantee that the labor and materials are free from defects, often for up to a year.

■ Arbitration clause. You and the contractor agree on and name a method of resolving disputes, such as binding arbitration.

■ Change-order procedures. If the contractor has provided you with a fixed-price bid, what happens if you decide to make changes to the plan in midcourse? This part of the contract spells out the answer. It lays out the steps to be taken for change orders and specifies a payment schedule for them. To prevent problems or misunderstandings, homeowners always should go to the contractor, not to a subcontractor, when requesting a change.

■ Release of liens. This provision assures homeowners that they won't be slapped with any liens, or charges upon their property to pay debts, that might be filed against the contractor.

Understanding Codes and Permits

If your remodeling project involves more than cosmetic changes, you'll probably need a building permit before the work begins—especially if you'll be making changes to your home's plumbing and electrical systems. If, however, your plans are limited to changing surface materials or replacing existing fixtures, you probably can get by without a permit. Check with your municipal and county building departments to see what is required where you live.

The main stipulation of a building permit is conformity to local building codes. Codes tend to be extensive and confusing, but they have an important purpose: They set minimum acceptability standards for structural integrity and sanitation-system design. They cover issues such as adequate ventilation, natural light, and electrical details. Conformity to applicable codes helps assure you of comfortable and safe living conditions. If you live in an incorporated part of a town or city, you must apply for a building permit, and a local building inspector will visit your site to ensure that you and your contractor are following all code requirements. Even if you live in a rural area where permits and inspection are not required, you should still be aware of code provisions and follow them.

Building codes vary by region, state, and locale, yet all codes have much in common. One provision that pertains to bathrooms, for example, is that a toilet must be located so that the center of its drain is at least 30 inches from any adjacent wall. This can present challenges in a tiny powder room or other cramped space.

➤ *If you divide your bath into compartments during remodeling, remember that building codes may specify, among other items, which way doors should swing and how much room you should leave around some fixtures, such as toilets.*

If you hire a general contractor, the contractor typically will obtain required permits. Be sure your construction contract specifies that the contractor and subcontractors will meet or exceed the code's minimum requirements.

Most local building departments require that contractors be state-licensed, which means (among other things) that they are familiar with codes. Once your building permit is issued, your contractor must arrange for timely inspections. If you act as your own general contractor, you will be responsible for your own work and that of any subcontractors. Some code officials require that you ask subcontractors to apply for their own permits unless you can show you are competent to perform the work involved.

Acting as Your Own General Contractor

If you have superb organizational skills, enjoy immersing yourself in lists and timetables, aren't easily bullied or buffaloed, and have plenty of time to devote to the project, you may want to act as your own general contractor. This can save you from paying the general contractor's fee, which is normally between 10 percent and 30 percent of the project's total cost. For a major remodeling project, this can amount to a great deal of money. Many people feel that this is money well spent, because good contractors work hard for their fees and remove many burdens from their clients' shoulders. But you may be an enthusiastic do-it-yourselfer and want to tackle the job.

Your job description as general contractor will include obtaining permits, arranging for inspections, selecting subcontractors, scheduling and supervising work, smoothing out disputes with or among subcontractors, monitoring the budget, and making payments to subcontractors and suppliers. As general contractor, you also will be involved in selecting, purchasing, and arranging delivery of materials.

To do the job well, you need to have basic knowledge of all the operations you'll be supervising. This may include additions or alterations to your home's electrical, plumbing, and mechanical systems (encompassing heating, ventilation, and air-conditioning). It also may mean changes to the structural framing, and interior and exterior wall materials and finishes. Study sections of the building codes that pertain to these areas. As general contractor, you are responsible for making sure jobs are done right. Your subcontractors could claim they were following your orders if some work is done poorly or incorrectly.

Unlike a professional contractor, you probably don't have a list of proven subcontractors to call upon. So you'll have to start from scratch by seeking recommendations from reliable sources. When possible, talk to former customers and look at examples of previous work. Determine as nearly as possible if each candidate has a good track record of work done well and on time.

As contractor, you also have to know the order in which various jobs usually are done, then schedule your subcontractors accordingly. The goal is to coordinate their schedules so as to avoid problems. On one hand, you don't want to have too many people on the building site stepping on each other's toes (this is especially critical in a small space such as a bathroom); on the other hand, you don't want to have long delays occur during construction. It often helps if your subcontractors have worked together before.

If you make any changes to your plans or specifications, be sure to tell all your subcontractors. You might think that one simple change affects only one trade, but it may affect others as well. The addition of a recessed cabinet, for example, might interfere with the plumber's vent stack and the electrician's wiring plan.

A smooth project requires that you have some technical knowledge, excellent organizational skills, and the ability to lead a team. As self-appointed general contractor, you're not only the homeowner—you're also the day-to-day boss at the remodeling site. It's up to you to communicate, return calls, show up for deliveries, inspect the site every day, and motivate the work crew.

What Subcontractors Will You Need?

Depending on how complex your remodeling is, your project may require several of the following specialized tradespeople.

Plumbing Contractor

If your remodeling plans include moving or adding any water lines, a licensed plumber will be necessary (in all likelihood, your local building code will require you hire one). These professionals install sewer and water lines, fixtures, and faucets. Like most other subcontractors, plumbers provide their own equipment and can help you find the necessary supplies. If you want special features—such as a certain type of faucet—buy it yourself in advance. Some plumbers also will install heating and cooling systems. If you require this work, be sure to ask your prospective plumber about it in advance.

Plumbers often play a larger role than other subcontractors in bathroom remodeling projects. For more on how to work with your plumber, see "When to Schedule a Plumber," page 110.

Framing Carpenter

If you plan to move walls—interior or exterior, partition or load-bearing—you'll need a qualified framing carpenter. These carpenters tear out and rebuild all affected rough framework, including floors, ceilings, and walls, so the site is ready for finish work. Framing carpenters also may install windows (see also "Glass Contractor," at right).

Drywall Contractor

Hanging and finishing gypsum wallboard, or drywall, are specialties unto themselves. Doing these jobs well is harder than it looks. It's often difficult to get large drywall installation companies to take on small jobs such as a remodeled bathroom.

You'll probably need to find a drywall "freelancer" (often these are people who work for large contractors and do moonlighting work on the side). Experienced and reliable drywall experts can be the hardest tradespeople to find.

Finish Carpenters

Some framing carpenters are also good at building or installing cabinets, built-in storage, trim, stair parts, doors, and windows; but this isn't always the case. You may have to look for a separate finish carpenter.

Electrical Contractor

An electrician usually is needed at two stages of construction: first, at the rough-in stage (right after you have made any necessary changes to the wall framing) when the wiring is rerouted or threaded through walls; second, after surface materials have been applied to finish out the job by installing outlets, switches, and lighting fixtures. Most electricians also will install wiring for additional telephones.

Glass Contractor

You can buy prefabricated windows from this contractor, who also will install your selections. In addition, a glass specialist will install glass doors, mirrors, shower doors, skylights, and any other glass products you require.

Miscellaneous Subcontractors

At this point, you may choose to hire other specialty contractors to finish your bath remodeling. Some additional contractors include painters, flooring installers, installers of solid-surface material (such as Corian), and interior decorators.

Working with Subcontractors

If you are acting as your own general contractor, you'll need to establish sound legal and professional relationships with your subcontractors. Avoiding problems through good communication is the key, but you'll also want to make provisions for resolving disputes should any arise. The following tips will help you work successfully with subcontractors.

■ Get all agreements between you and your contractors in writing. Well-written contracts are invaluable. If you need to, enlist the services of a real estate lawyer who has experience in writing and reviewing construction contracts.

■ Try to be present for as much of the work as you can; at least be present for all subcontractors' initial visits, until you feel you can trust them.

■ Good communication between you and each subcontractor, and also between your subcontractors, is vital to a successful project.

■ Delayed deliveries of materials can wreak havoc with subcontractors and scheduling. Order your materials early. Insist on timely deliveries. Make sure you have a protected, secure place for storing materials. And check each delivery carefully so you can send any damaged goods back on the same truck.

When to Schedule a Plumber

In bathroom remodeling projects, the plumber often plays a larger role than other subcontractors. Your plumber probably will need to make more than one visit to your home during the course of the project.

At the Start

You'll want to have a plumber come in at the beginning to disconnect the toilet, sinks, and shower faucets. If you live in a house that was built before 1970, the supply lines to your plumbing fixtures may not have individual shut-off valves. Be sure to install these now, so you can tear the room apart without having to turn off the water to the whole house.

Pay careful attention to any advice your plumber has to offer as you tear out the old bathroom. Ask about the locations of pipes that may be hidden under the floor and in the walls. The last thing you'll want to do is pay emergency rates (and face the cleanup) after you've damaged a water-supply or drain line.

At this time, you also may want the plumber to temporarily remove any pipes that would get in your way as you rebuild the walls.

Roughing In

After everything has been torn out, cleaned up, and any new wall framing built, have your plumber come back to replace any old galvanized supply pipes with copper, as well as any pipes that are corroded or partially blocked with deposits. This is the time to replace the tub, if necessary, and to rough in necessary pipes for the new bathroom's water-supply and drain, waste, and vent systems.

Finishing Up

Once most of the other work has been completed, the plumber should make a final visit. After the plumber has set the new fixtures, hooked them up, and installed the new faucets, you can begin to enjoy your newly remodeled bathroom.

Doing Some of the Work Yourself

Whether or not you act as your own general contractor, you may want to save money by doing some of the work yourself. It's best to limit yourself to projects you can handle.

■ Demolition work can be a fun family project. Remember to observe proper safety measures. These may include wearing dust masks, eye protection, gloves, and other protective clothing.

■ Hiring people to clean up waste can be expensive. You may wind up paying a skilled carpenter a high hourly rate just to push a broom. Doing this work yourself will keep labor costs down. This, too, can be a good family project.

■ Painting or finishing woodwork is a good job for homeowners who are willing to invest the time to do it right.

■ Installing surface finishes, such as floor coverings and ceramic tile, can be done after the subcontractors leave. Be sure you're up to the job. If you botch the installation of a large piece of vinyl flooring, for example, you'll be out more money than you would have saved by doing it yourself. Tile may be more labor-intensive, but each piece costs less if you make a mistake.

■ Some electrical and plumbing rough-in work is difficult to coordinate with other trades. You may want to limit yourself to doing the finish work, such as installing plumbing and lighting fixtures, outlets, and switches. Before doing any plumbing or electrical work yourself, check to see if local building codes require that such work be done by licensed professionals.

Coping with Chaos

Inevitably, remodeling a bathroom will disrupt your family. If you take steps to reduce both the mess and the stress, everyone will benefit.

■ Before the project begins, secure a mechanic's lien waiver so you won't be held responsible if your contractor doesn't pay the subcontractors. Consult an attorney or a banker for details. Taking this simple precaution will save you anxiety.

■ In preparation for construction, clean out the bathroom and nearby areas. Remove all furniture, bathroom supplies, toiletry items, rugs, and accessories. Don't expect the construction crew to work around your belongings.

■ Block adjacent doors and hallways by hanging sheets of plastic. Tape the plastic to door frames, walls, and ceilings to prevent fine dust from drifting into other rooms. If your project involves removing any plaster, sprinkle the plastic sheets with water before removing the plaster to keep the dust down.

■ To protect your floors, cover them with plastic, sheets, or old carpet. Put a doormat outside the bathroom to help the crew avoid tracking dust and debris throughout the house.

■ If the only bathroom in the house will be out of commission for a while, set up temporary accommodations that include a chemical toilet, washup facilities, and portable shower. Borrow or buy camping equipment that will provide for basic needs.

■ Give thought to the seasonal timing of your project. It's easier to cope with remodeling during warmer times of year, when your family can go outdoors for relief from the noise and mess.

Index

Numbers in **bold** typeface indicate pages where the item listed is photographed.

A–B

Accessible baths, **29**
Adding a bath, 10, **11**, **52-59**
Architects, 43, 59
Attic baths, **11**, **52**, **74-75**
Bath designers, 43, 59
Bath sizes and types, 7
Bidets, 100
Budget, 14, 66, 72, 74. *See also* Costs
Building codes and permits, 36, 56, 58, 59, 107
Bump-outs, **56-57**

C

Cabinets, 88, 91, **102-103**. *See also* Storage; Vanities
Carpenters, 109
Carpet, 85
Children's baths, **8**, **21-23**
Clearances, 29, 34-35
Color schemes, 30, 31
Compartmented baths, **8**, **21**, 35, 49
Computer-aided design, 61
Contracting, do-it-yourself, 108-110
Contractors, 104-107, 109
Contracts, 106
Cosmetic center, 31
Costs
    countertops, 88-89, 91
    cutting, 78
    estimating, 76-81
    fixtures, 14, 79, 95, 99
    flooring, 84-85, 91
    glass block, 87
    regional variations, 79
    tile, 84, 89
    tub and shower surrounds, 90
    See also Budget
Countertops, 48, 88-**89**, 91

D-H

Design
    notebook, 43
    professionals, 32, 43, 59, 104
    trends, 4, 14
Disabled, bathrooms for, **29**
Drywall contractors, 109
Electrical systems
    contractors, 109
    outlets, 6, 23, 31, 42
Exhaust fans, 36-37
Expanding a bath, 10, **21**, 44, 51
Facelifts for baths, 10, 44, 46-**47**
Faucets, 37, 95, 99
Fiberglass surrounds, 90

Fixtures, 14, 34, 79, 92, 101. *See also* specific fixtures
Flooring, 42, 84-85, 91
Full baths, 7, **24**, 53
Glass block, **8**, 36, 87, **98**
Granite, 89
Half baths, 7, 52, **54-55**

I-O

Insulation, 36
Laminate, 88
Lighting
    compartmented baths, **8**
    fixtures, 38-**39**
    around mirrors, **32**, 38
    skylights, 49
    in small baths, 46
Marble, 85, 89
Master baths, **9**
Materials
    cabinets, 88
    in children's baths, **22**
    choosing, 82, 91
    countertops, 88-**89**
    design trends, 14
    flooring, 84-**85**
    natural, **27**
    sinks, 94
    tub and shower surrounds, 90
    walls, 86-**87**
Measurements, 7, 34-35, 52
Medicine chests, 40
Mirrors, **24**, 31, 38, **50**
Moisture solutions, 36-37

P-R

Paint, 86-87
Planning, 6, 7, 14, 60-61
Plumbing
    basics, 12-13
    contractors, 109
    layouts, 34
    scheduling, 65, 110
Powder rooms, 7, **18-20**
Privacy, 28, 36
Remodeling
    journal, 72-73
    levels, 10, **11**, 44
    living with, **68**-72, 102, 111
    trends, 4, **8-9**, 14
Renovating, 44, **48**, 49
Resale value, 4, 6, 14, 74, 78, 79

S

Safety, 22, 23, 42
Showerheads, **27**, **28**, 37, 99
Showers
    in accessible baths, **29**
    choosing, **98-99**
    measurements, 35, 99
    safety considerations, 42
    surrounds, 90
Sinks, 34, 46, **94**-95
Sketches, 60-61

Skylights, 49, **52**, **57**
Small baths, 10, **11**, **18**, 35, 46
Solid-surface materials, 89, 90
Space for bath, finding, 10, **52-54**
Spas, 9, **56**
Storage, 14, **40**, **41**, 46, 49. *See also* Cabinets
Subcontractors, 65, 66, 108-110

T-U

Three-quarter baths, 7
Tile
    countertops, 89
    floors, **62-63**, 84, **86**
    installation tips, 70
    tub and shower surrounds, 90
    wall, 87, **90**
Toilets, **27**, 35, **63**, **100**
Trends in design and remodeling, 4, **8-9**, 14
Tubs
    buying tips, 96
    claw-foot, **16-17**, **25**
    resurfacing, 46
    surrounds, 90
    for two, 28
    whirlpool, 14, 28, **92-93**, 96, **97**

V-Z

Vanities
    in accessible baths, **29**
    heights, 35
    storage, **40**, **41**
    types, 94-95
Ventilation, 36-37
Walls and wall coverings, **23**, **54**, 86-87, 91
Water
    conservation, 37, 100
    hardness, 37
Window coverings, 36, **74-75**
Windows, 14, 36, 109
Wood surfaces, **85**, 87, 89

U.S. Units to Metric Equivalents		
To convert from	Multiply by	To get
Inches	25.4	Millimeters (mm)
Inches	2.54	Centimeters (cm)
Feet	30.48	Centimeters (cm)
Feet	0.3048	Meters (m)
Cubic Feet	28.316	Liters (l)

Metric Units to U.S. Equivalents		
To convert from	Multiply by	To get
Millimeters	0.0394	Inches
Centimeters	0.3937	Inches
Centimeters	0.0328	Feet
Meters	3.2808	Feet
Liters	0.0353	Cubic Feet